Bathroom Bits

hacked by
Rick D'Elia

outskirtspress
DENVER, COLORADO

Outskirts Press, Inc.
http://www.outskirtspress.com

ISBN: 978-1-4327-9625-9

Outskirts Press and the "OP" logo are trademarks belonging to Outskirts Press, Inc.

PRINTED IN THE UNITED STATES OF AMERICA

Acknowledgements

Special thanks to Paul D'Angelo, Kevin Kearney, Mark Wilde, Tom Cotter, Dobie Maxwell and Lou Salvino for always sending me new street jokes, fresh off the presses. In fact, at least half of the jokes included in this book I got from them. I probably should cut them in on the profits but I'm sure a sincere "thank you" is all the compensation they would ever ask for. I certainly hope that blanket statement holds up at the trial!

Much love to my friends Tara Johnson, Candy & George Campbell, and Diana Alouise (my canine son's mother) for all your support personally and professionally and for always being in my corner. Cheers!

To Woody & Linda Cunrod; just 'cuz I ain't "kin folk" no more, you shouldn't be deprived of dirty jokes!

Additional Credits:

Photography by:	Ramsey Etchison
	(Ramseyetchison@gmail.com)
Cover Design by:	Nola Rocco
Bathroom Location:	Moody's Bistro, Bar & Beats
Illustrations by:	Paul D'Angelo
Formatting by:	Jeff Carlson
Publishing Consultant:	Jerry Banks
Cover Girl:	Diana Alouise
	www.DianaAlouise.com
Wardrobe Provided By:	Marilyn's Catwalk, Truckee, CA

Table of Contents

Introduction: "Tell Me A Joke!"

Scenario # 1

<u>Person</u>: You're a comedian? Tell me a joke!

<u>Comic</u>: I don't really know many jokes.

<u>Person</u>: What kind of comedian doesn't know any jokes?

<u>Comic</u>: The kind that write their own material. And Carrot Top.

<u>Person</u>: Huh?

<u>Comic</u>: Comedians don't really tell "street jokes," we do "bits."

<u>Person</u>: What's the difference?

<u>Comic</u>: Okay, a "street joke" is a term used to describe a standard, public domain joke. Comedians write "bits" or "chunks,"

drawing from personal experiences and then exaggerate for comedic effect. Do you see the difference?

Person: No. And I think Carrot Top is hilarious.

Comic: Well, he doesn't tell jokes either. He uses props which, technically, are his "bits."

Person: Are you going to tell me a friggin' joke or not?

Comic: Fine. Two Jews walked into a bar... and bought it!

Scenario #2

Person: What do you do for work?

Comic: I'm a comedian.

Person: Really? Are you any good? You don't seem that funny; funny looking maybe but hey... maybe I should be a comedian too? (laughs to himself) So do you make a lot of money? I'm just asking 'cuz I've never heard of you so... anyway, what's your shtick? I could use a good laugh. I had a crazy week ya' know? You should come to my office some time – now that's where you could get some good material. This guy Larry in sales is a friggin' riot! (*laughs to himself*) Speaking of Larry, do you like Larry the Cable Guy? Now he's funny! "Get 'er dun!" (*laughs to himself*) What's your catchphrase? Only the good comics have a catchphrase...

Most comedians find themselves in these scenarios on

a regular basis. Now, when people ask what I do for work I just tell them I'm an accountant; that way there's usually no follow-up, only a nod and a perfunctory "Hmm, that's nice." Telling someone you're a comedian opens you up for a barrage of questions that I can't imagine people in other professions are routinely asked. Would you ever tell a school teacher, "Really? You don't seem that smart. How much do you make? Are you any good? Teach me a lesson!" In my opinion, asking someone about money, competency, and a sample of their work should only be reserved for hookers.

Street Jokes

One of the cool perks of being in the comedy business is having access to the world's best street jokes. Not the lame ones you get from a gag book or the ones your idiot co-worker has been quoting from Reader's Digest since he started there. These are the jokes comics pass around to each other. If you can make a comic laugh, it's either really funny or you're a booking agent getting your ass kissed.

Anyone can rattle off a street joke and usually get as big a laugh as a comedian will with a well-honed bit. This sucks if you're a comedian. I guess street jokes probably have a higher success rate because they instantly reach a broader audience. You don't have to pull people into your world or have them buy into to your character. Plus, telling a street joke doesn't require a two-drink minimum.

So if not the comedian, where do street jokes come from? I've had this conversation with a million comics and no one seems to know. I've heard rumors that they come from bored prisoners sitting around in their cells trying to outwit each other. I don't support this theory. I've never done any jail time but I'd wager most inmates spend the better chunk of their days trying to either avoid or incite shower rape. I could be wrong. Another theory is they hail from the financial wizards who run Wall Street. (Hence the word, "street") Ever meet a banker with a sense of humor? Didn't think so.

Where these street jokes originate is inconsequential; the bottom line is that they're really funny. Whoever out there is whipping up these gems, please keep 'em coming! To you the reader: keep this book in your bathroom. I guarantee it'll help you get your business done more efficiently than a cup of coffee and besides, it's healthier for you too! As the cliché goes, "Laughter is the best medicine!" (Unless, of course, you have syphilis. That's a tough one to laugh off. Just sayin'…)

Cheers,

Rick D'Elia
CPA

P.S. Some of you will find many of these jokes crude, politically incorrect and racy. If you offend easily, before complaining to the ACLU, please consider the following facts:

1) Don't kill the messenger! I didn't write these jokes. I just compiled, tweaked & edited them.

2) You are a fag!

1

Men vs Women

John Grey wrote a popular book in the 90's called, Men are from Mars: Women are from Venus. This book sold millions of copies while simultaneously adding to the existing divide between men and women. I read this book - it was completely useless; just an obvious ploy to exploit lovelorn people in a futile attempt to explain our differences. The fact is we have always been and always will be different and no one will ever be able to explain why. I cover that in great depth in my next book, *Men Suck! Women Suck! We Both Like to Fuck… Best of Luck!!!*

The following jokes slam women and men equally. I started out with the male perspective first, not because the jokes are funnier or the message more important, I simply did it so the women would be able to have the last word.

After all, I want to keep it real & true to life!

He Said...

"Women will never be equal to men until they can
walk down the street with a bald head and a
beer gut, and still think they are sexy."

A woman is standing nude, looking in the bedroom mirror.
She is not happy with what she sees and says to her husband, "I
feel horrible; I look old, fat and ugly. I really need you to pay
me a compliment." He replies, "Well, your eyesight is damn near
perfect." And that's how the fight started...

My wife was hinting about what she wanted for our upcom-
ing anniversary. She said, "I want something shiny that goes from
0 to 200 in about 3 seconds." I bought her a scale. And that's how
the fight started...

One year, a husband decided to buy his mother-in-law a
cemetery plot as a Christmas gift. The next year, he didn't buy
her a gift. When she asked him why, he replied, "Well, you still
haven't used the gift I bought you last year!" And that's how the
fight started...

A woman goes to the doctor all black and blue. The doctor
asked what happened and she says, "Doc, I don't know what to
do; every time my husband comes home drunk he beats me to
a pulp."

The doctor says, "I have a sure-fire cure for that. The next
time your husband comes home drunk, just take a glass of sweet
tea and start swishing it in your mouth, but don't swallow. Just
keep swishing it around your mouth until he goes to bed in his
drunken stupor."

A week later she came back looking radiant, "Doctor, what a brilliant idea! Every time my husband came home drunk, I swished my mouth with sweet tea and he never laid a hand on me!"

The doctor says, "You see how much keeping your mouth shut helps?"

A woman, pregnant with her first child, went to her obstetrician's office. After the exam, she shyly said, "My husband wants me to ask you--" The doctor interrupts, "I know, I know..." placing a reassuring hand on her shoulder. "I get asked that all the time. Sex is fine until late in the pregnancy."

"No, that's not it," she confessed. "He wants to know if I can still mow the lawn."

A woman met a man in a bar. They talk, connect, and then leave together. When they get back to his place, she sees that one wall of his bedroom is completely filled with teddy bears. There are three shelves with dozens of these adorable bears. It was clear to her that he had taken some time to lovingly arrange them. She was immediately touched by the amount of thought he had put into organizing the display. The smaller teddy bears were all along the bottom shelf, bigger bears covering the length of the middle, and biggest bears were across the top. She found herself wildly attracted to this sensitive, yet extremely masculine guy with all the teddy bears.

They share a bottle of wine, snuggle up and make small talk. After awhile, she finds herself thinking, "Oh my God! I think this guy could be the one! Maybe I've found the future father of my children!" She turns and kisses him on the lips. He responds gently. The passion builds and they rip off each other's clothes and begin to make hot, passionate, steamy love.

After an intense, explosive night of raw passion with this

sensitive, beautiful man, they lie together in the afterglow. The woman rolls over, strokes his chest and asks coyly, "Well... how was that?" The guy smiles at her, brushes the hair from her face, looks deeply into her eyes and says, "Help yourself to any prize from the middle shelf."

A plane is passing through a severe storm; awful turbulence, a wing is struck by lightning... One woman completely loses it and starts screaming, "I'm too young to die! No one has ever made me really feel like a real woman! Please, is there anyone on this plane who can make me feel like a real woman, at least just one time before I meet my maker?"

For a moment, there is silence. Then, a gorgeous, tall, well built man stands up in the rear of the plane. "I can make you feel like a woman," he says. He starts walking up the aisle, unbuttoning his shirt one button at a time. The woman is breathing heavily in anticipation as he approaches and removes his shirt. Muscles ripple across his chest as he reaches her, and holds his shirt to the trembling woman, and whispers: "Iron this!"

Abdul is walking along the Gaza Strip, trips over a bottle, and a genie pops out. "Wow, I was trapped in that bottle for centuries. As is customary, I'll grant you one wish; anything in the world!"

So Abdul pulls out a map of the Middle East and shows it to the genie. "Could you please instill peace here?" The genie looks at the map, "Uh, well... the thing is, the fighting and wars were going on long before I got trapped in the bottle. Sorry but there's nothing I can do."

Abdul thinks for a minute. "Okay, then can you grant that my wife gives me a blowjob at least once a month?" The genie says, "Let's have a look at that map again..."

I never figured out why the sexual urge of men and women differ so much or why men think with their heads and women with their hearts. One evening, my girlfriend and I were in bed, the passion was heating up and she eventually said, "I don't feel like it, I just want you to hold me." I said, "WHAT??!! What's this all about?!" Then she uttered the words every guy dreads... "You're just not in touch with my emotional needs as a woman enough for me to satisfy your physical needs as a man. Can't you just love me for who I am and not what I do for you in the bedroom?" Realizing that nothing was going to happen that night, I went to sleep.

The next day I skipped work to spend time with her. We went out to a nice lunch and then shopping at a big department store. I watched her she try on several different, very expensive outfits. She couldn't decide which one to take, so I told her we'd just buy them all. She wanted new shoes to compliment her new clothes, so I said, "Lets get a pair for each outfit." We went to the jewelry department where she picked out a pair of diamond earrings. Next she tried on a tennis bracelet and she doesn't even play tennis. I said, "That's fine, honey. Anything you want!" She was so excited. Smiling with anticipation, she finally said, "This is all dear, let's go to the cashier."

I could hardly contain myself when I blurted out, "No honey, I don't feel like it." Her face went blank as her jaw dropped with a baffled, "WHAT?" I then said, "Honey! I just want you to hold this stuff for a while. You're just not in touch with my financial needs as a man enough for me to satisfy your shopping needs as a woman." And just when she had this look like she was going to kill me, I added, "Why can't you just love me for who I am and not for the things I buy you?"

Apparently I'm not having sex tonight either....but at least that bitch knows I'm smarter than her!

Sexist Woman Q&A

Q: What is the definition of a woman?
A: A life support system for a vagina.

Q: What's the difference between a wife & a girlfriend?
A: About 45 lbs.

Q: Why haven't they sent a woman to the moon?
A: It doesn't need cleaning.

Q: Why do brides wear white?
A: So the dishwasher will match the fridge & stove.

Q: Why are women's feet smaller than man's?
A: So they can stand closer to the oven.

Q: How do you know when it's time to wash dishes and clean the house?
A: Look inside your pants; if you have a penis, it's not time.

Q: How can you tell when a woman is about to say something intelligent?
A: When she begins a sentence with; "A man once told me..."

Q: What's the smartest thing ever to come out a woman's mouth?
A: Einstein's cock.

Q: If your wife keeps coming out of the kitchen to nag you, what have you done wrong?
A: Made her chain too long.

Q: What does it mean if you're wife is in bed with you, gasping for air and calling your name?
A: You didn't hold the pillow long enough.

Q: How can you tell if your wife is dead?
A: The sex is the same but the dishes pile up.

Q: What do you say to a woman with two black eyes?
A: Nothing, she's already heard it twice.

Q: What did the battered woman do when she came back from the hospital?
A: The dishes.

Q: How many women does it take to screw in a light bulb?
A: One; she just holds it up and waits for the world to revolve around her.

Q: What do you call a female Humpty-Dumpty?
A: Humpty Cunt.

Q: What's the difference between a woman and sheep?
A: Sheep don't get upset if you fuck her sister.

Q: Why did God create yeast infections?
A: So women know what it's like to live with an irritating cunt once in a while too.

Q: Why do men pay more for car insurance?
A: 'Cuz women don't get blowjobs while they're driving.

Q: Why do they call it PMS?
A: Mad Cow Disease was already taken.

Q: What's a mixed feeling?
A: When you see your mother-in-law backing off a cliff in your new car.

Q: How is a woman like a condom?
A: Both spend more time in your wallet than on your dick.

Q: How many men does it take to open a beer?
A: None. It should be opened by the time she brings it.

Q: What's the definition of making love?
A: It's what she's doing while you're fucking her.

Q: How do you fix a woman's watch?
A: You don't. There is a clock on the oven.

Q: Why do men fart more than women?
A: Be cause women can't shut up long enough to build up the required pressure.

Q: Your dog is barking at the back door, your wife is yelling at the front; who do you let in?
A: The dog, of course. He'll shut up once you let him in.

Q: What's worse than a male chauvinist pig?
A: A woman who won't do what she's told.

Q: What food diminishes a woman's sex drive by 99%?
A: Wedding Cake.

Q: Why do men die before their wives?
A: They want to.

Q: Why couldn't Helen Keller drive?
A: She was a woman.

Q: What should you do if you find a woman lying in a ditch at the side of the road?
A: Ask her why she left the kitchen.

Q: Why did the feminist cross the road?
A: To suck my dick.

She Said…

<u>A Wife's Perfect Breakfast</u>

She's sitting at the table with her gourmet coffee…
Her son is on the cover of the Wheaties box.
Her daughter is on the cover of Business Week.
Her boyfriend is on the cover of Playgirl.
And her husband is on the back of a milk carton.

A couple is lying in bed. He says, "I'm going to make you the happiest woman in the world!" She says, "I'll miss you…"

A man said to his wife one day, "I don't know how you can be so stupid and so beautiful at the same time." The wife responded, "Allow me to explain. God made me beautiful so you'd be attracted to me and He made me stupid so I'd be attracted to you!"

Once upon a time there was a female brain cell which by mistake happened to end up in a man's head. She looked around nervously, but it was all empty and quiet. "Hello?" she called, but there was no answer. "Is there anyone here?" she called a little louder, but still no answer. The female brain cell started to feel alone and scared, so she yelled at the top of her lungs, "HELLO! IS THERE ANYONE HERE?" Then she heard a faint voice from far, far away say, "We're down here."

Relatives were gathered in the hospital waiting room when finally, the doctor came in. "I'm afraid I am the bearer of bad news; the only hope left for your loved one is a brain transplant. It's a risky, experimental procedure and you'll have to pay for the brain yourselves." The family sat silent as they absorbed the news. After a while, someone asked, "Well, how much does a brain cost?"

The doctor quickly responded, "$5000 for a male brain, and $200 for a female brain."

The moment turned awkward. Men in the room tried not to smirk and avoided eye contact with the women. One man suddenly blurted out, "So, why is the male brain so much more?"

The doctor replied, "It's just standard pricing procedure. We have to mark down the price of the female brains, because they've been used."

A couple drove down a country road for several miles,

not saying a word after an earlier argument. Neither of them wanted to concede their position. As they passed a barnyard of mules, goats, and pigs, the husband rather sarcastically asked, "Relatives of yours?"

"Yep," she confidently replied, "in-laws."

A man escapes from prison where he's been for 15 years. He breaks into a house and finds a young couple in bed. He grabs the guy out of bed and ties him to a chair. After tying the girl he gets on top of her and kisses her neck. Then he goes to the bathroom and, while he's in there, the husband tells his wife, "Listen, this guy's an escaped convict. He probably hasn't seen a woman in years. I saw how he kissed your neck. If he wants sex, don't resist, don't complain; just do whatever he wants you to no matter how much it disgusts you. If you make him angry he'll probably wind up killing the both of us! So be strong honey, I love you!!!"

She responds, "He wasn't kissing my neck. He was whispering in my ear. He told me he was gay, thought you were cute and asked if we had any Vaseline. I told him it was in the bathroom. So, be strong honey. I love you too!!!"

A middle-aged couple had two beautiful daughters but always wanted a son. They decided to try one last time for the son they always dreamed of. The wife got pregnant and delivered a healthy baby boy. The joyful father rushed to the nursery to see his new son but was horrified by the ugliest child he'd ever seen. He told his wife, "There's no way I can be the father of this baby. Look at the two beautiful daughters I fathered! Have you been fooling around behind my back?"

The wife smiled sweetly and replied, "No, not this time!"

One day my housework-challenged husband decided to wash his sweatshirt. Seconds after he stepped into the laundry room, he shouted, "Dear, what setting do I use on the washing machine?"

"It really depends honey," I replied. "What does it say on your shirt?"

He yelled back, "University of Oklahoma." And they say blondes are dumb...

"It's just too hot to wear clothes today!" said the husband as he stepped out of the shower. "Honey, what do you suppose the neighbors would think if I mowed the lawn like this?"

She replied, "That I married you for your money!"

It was the mailman's last day after 35 years of delivering in the same neighborhood. When he arrived at the first house he was greeted by a family who congratulated him and gave him a wonderful gift bag. At the second house he was presented with a box of fine cigars and a tackle box full of terrific fishing lures, lines, sinkers and bobbers. This continued all day.

Finally, at the last house, he was met by a strikingly beautiful woman wearing nothing but a sexy negligee. She took him by the hand and led him up the stairs to the bedroom where she ravaged him with the most passionate love he had ever experienced. When they finished, they went downstairs where she fixed him a giant breakfast of eggs, potatoes, ham, sausage, blueberry waffles, and fresh-squeezed orange juice. After they finished eating, she poured him a cup of fresh ground coffee and then slipped a dollar bill under the coffee mug.

He asked "This was all just too amazing for words, but what's the dollar for?"

She said, "Well last night, I told my husband that today would be your last day, and that we should do something special for you. He said, "Fuck him; give him a dollar!" Then she smiled, "The breakfast was my idea."

A man boarded an airplane in New Orleans with a box of frozen crabs. A female crew member took the box and promised to put it in the crew's refrigerator. The man rudely told her he was holding her personally responsible for the crabs staying frozen. He then proceeded to rant about what would happen to her if she negligently let them thaw out.

Shortly before landing in New York, she announced over the intercom to the entire cabin, "Would the gentleman who gave me the crabs in New Orleans, please raise your hand?"

Not one hand went up. So she took the crabs home and ate them herself. Some men just never learn!

Dan was a single guy living at home with his father and working in the family business. When he found out he was going to inherit a fortune when his sickly father died, he decided he needed a wife with which to share his fortune. One evening at an investment meeting he spotted the most beautiful woman he had ever seen. Her natural beauty took his breath away.

"I may look like just an ordinary man," he said to her, but in just a few years, my father will die, and I will be the only one to inherit his entire $200 million fortune and estate."

Impressed, the woman obtained his business card and three days later, she became his stepmother. The moral? Women are so much better at financial planning than men!

A woman rushes into her house one morning and yells to her husband, "Sam, pack up your stuff. I just won the lottery!" Excited, he asks, "Shall I pack for warm weather or cold?"

"Whatever… just as long as you're out of the house by noon!"

Three guys were sitting in a bar. The first guy said, "My wife is so dumb, she carries a garage-door clicker in her car and we don't even have an automatic garage door." The second guy said, "My wife is so dumb, she has a cellular phone antenna on her car and she doesn't even have a cellular phone." The third guy said, "My wife is so dumb, she carries a purse full of rubbers and she doesn't even have a dick."

A man and his wife were having problems and were giving each other the silent treatment. Suddenly, he realized that the next day he would need his wife to wake him at 5:00 AM for an early morning business flight. Not wanting to break the silence first and lose the battle, he wrote on a piece of paper, "Please wake me at 5:00 AM." He left it where he knew she'd find it.

The next morning, he woke up, only to discover it was 9:00 AM and he had missed his flight. Furious, he was about to go and see why his wife didn't wake him when he noticed a piece of paper by the bed that read, "It is 5:00 AM. Wake up!!!" The moral? Men are not equipped for these kinds of contests!

Sexist Man Q&A

Q. What do you call the useless piece of skin on the end of a man's penis?
A. His body.

Q: Why do men take showers instead of baths?
A: 'Cuz pissing in a bath is gross...

Q: What's the difference between a new husband and a new dog?
A: After a year, the dog is still excited to see you.

Q: What makes men chase women they have no intention of marrying?
A: The same urge that makes dogs chase cars they have no intention of driving.

Q. How can you tell when a man is well hung?
A. When you can just barely slip your finger in between his neck and the noose.

Q. How do men define a "50/50" relationship?
A. We cook-they eat; we clean-they dirty; we iron-they wrinkle.

Q. How do men exercise on the beach?
A. By sucking in their stomachs every time they see a bikini.

Q. How do you get a man to stop biting his nails?
A. Make him wear shoes.

Q. How do you keep your husband from reading your e-mail?
A. Rename the mail folder "Instruction Manuals."

Q. How does a man show he's planning for the future?
A. He buys two cases of beer instead of one.

Q. What makes a man think about a candlelight dinner?
A. A power failure.

Q. What should you give a man who has everything?
A. A woman to show him how to work it.

Q. What do men and mascara have in common?
A. They both run at the first sign of emotion.

Q. What do men and pantyhose have in common?
A. They either cling, run, or don't fit right in the crotch!

Q. What do you instantly know about a well-dressed man?
A. His wife is good at picking out clothes.

Q. What's a man's definition of a romantic evening?
A. Sex.

Q. What's the best way to force a man to do sit ups?
A. Put the remote control between his toes.

Q. Why do men like smart women?
A. Opposites attract.

Q. Why do men name their penises?
A. Because they don't like the idea of having a stranger make 90% of their decisions.

Q. Why do men need instant replay on TV sports?
A. Because after 30 seconds they forget what happened.

Q. Why do men whistle when they're sitting on the toilet?

A. Because it helps them remember which end they need to wipe.

Q. What do men and sperm have in common?

A. They both have one in a million chance of becoming a human being.

2

Love & Marriage

I am an expert on this subject. While I've never actually been married, I have dated many married women and I can tell you exactly what they want: Anything but their husbands! I have been close though. I actually did spend 7 faithful years with the same woman. People would constantly say to me, "Seven years? Wow, do I hear wedding bells?" My reply was always genuine, "Wedding bells? I dunno… I can't hear a damn thing over her nagging all the friggin' time!"

All kidding aside; I'm not kidding. I'll let the experts speak for themselves…

Great Minds Think Alike
In the beginning, God created the earth and rested.
Then God created Man and rested.
Then God created Woman.
Since then, neither God nor Man has rested.

Women inspire us to do great things and prevent us from achieving them. - *Dumas*

The great question, which I have not been able to answer is, "What do women want?" - *Freud*

When a man steals your wife, there is no better revenge than to let him keep her. - *Guitry*

My wife and I were happy for twenty years. Then we met. - *Rodney Dangerfield*

A good wife always forgives her husband when she's wrong. - *Milton Berle*

The most effective way to remember your wife's birthday is to forget it once... *Anonymous*

You know what I did before I married? Anything I wanted to. - *Henny Youngman*

I had some words with my wife; and she had some paragraphs with me. - *Anonymous*

After marriage, husband and wife become two sides of a coin; they just can't face each other but still they stay together. – *Joshi*

Marriage is an institution in which a man loses his Bachelor's Degree and a woman gets her Masters! - *Anonymous*

By all means marry. If you get a good wife, you'll be happy. If you get a bad one, you'll become a philosopher. - *Socrates*

Some people ask the secret of our long marriage: We take time to go to a restaurant two times a week, a little candle-light, dinner, soft music and dancing. She goes Tuesdays, I go Fridays. - *Henny Youngman*

There's a way of transferring funds that is even faster than electronic banking. It's called marriage. - *James Holt McGavran*

I've had bad luck with both my wives. The first one left me and the second one didn't. - *Patrick Murray*

Definition of a bachelor: A man who's missed the opportunity to make a woman's life miserable. - *Anonymous*

Marriage is like going to a restaurant; you order what you want and when you see what the guy next to you has, you wish you ordered that. - *Anonymous*

Two secrets to keep your marriage brimming: Whenever you're wrong, admit it, and whenever you're right, shut up. - *Nash*

Can't live with 'em; can't live without 'em!

First Guy says proudly: "My wife's an angel!"
Second Guy: "You're lucky. Mine's still alive."

Q: Why is it so hard for a woman to find a sensitive, caring, good-looking man?
A: Because those men already have boyfriends.

Q: What do you call a woman who knows where her husband is at all times?
A: A widow.

A man ran a classified ad: "Wife wanted." The next day he received a hundred letters. They all said the same thing: "You can have mine."

While attending a Marriage Seminar dealing with communication, Tom and his wife Grace listened to the instructor, "It is essential that husbands and wives know each other's likes and dislikes." He addressed the man, "Can you name your wife's favorite flower?"

Tom leaned over, touched his wife's arm gently and whispered, "Its Pillsbury isn't it?"

This guy is sitting at home alone when he hears a knock on the front door. There are two sheriff's deputies there; he asks if there is a problem. One of the deputies asks if he is married, and if so, can he see a picture of his wife. The guy says "sure" and shows him a picture of his wife.

The sheriff says, "Yeah, that's her. I'm sorry to tell you sir, but it looks like your wife's been hit by a truck." The guy says, "I know, but she has a great personality and is an excellent cook!"

A guy just finished reading a book titled; *You Can Be the Man of Your House!* He stormed to in the kitchen and announced, "From now on, you need to know that I am the man of this house and my word is law. Tonight you will prepare me a gourmet meal, and when I'm finished eating, you will serve me a sumptuous dessert. After dinner, we are going upstairs to have the kind of sex that I want. Afterwards, you're going to draw me a bath. You will wash my back, towel me dry, and bring me my robe. Then, you will massage my feet and hands. And tomorrow, guess who's going to dress me and comb my hair?"

She replied, "The fucking funeral director would be my first guess!"

One morning a man noticed a most unusual funeral procession approaching the nearby cemetery. A long black hearse was followed by a second long black hearse about 50 feet behind the first one. Behind the second hearse was a man walking a dog on a leash. Behind him, a short distance back, were about 200 men walking single file.

His curiosity got the best of him so he approached the man walking the dog and said, "I am so sorry for your loss, and I know now is a bad time to disturb you, but I've never seen a service like this. Whose funeral is it?'

"My wife's." the man sadly replied.

"What happened to her?"

"My dog attacked and killed her."

"But who is in the second hearse?"

"My mother-in-law. She was trying to help my wife when t he dog turned on her."

A poignant and thoughtful moment of silence passed before he asked, "Forgive my timing but can I borrow your dog?"

"Get in line."

One day John came home with a most unusual purchase: a robot he claimed was actually a lie detector. His wife Marsha was not impressed. At 5:30 that evening, their 11 year-old son Tommy came home from school over 2 hours late.

"Where have you been? Why are you so late?" asked John.

"My friends and I went to the library to work on an extra credit project." said Tommy. The robot then walked around the table and slapped Tommy, knocking him off of his chair.

"Son, this robot is a lie detector; now tell us where you really were after school!"

"Okay, we went to Bobby's house and watched a movie." said Tommy.

"What did you watch?" asked Marsha.

"The Ten Commandments." answered Tommy. The robot immediately slapped him, knocking him off his chair again. With his lip quivering, he got up and said, "I am sorry I lied. We really watched a movie called Ass Bandits."

John said, "I am ashamed of you son. When I was your age, I never lied to my parents!"

Then the robot walked around to John and whacked him, knocking him to the ground.

Marsha doubled over in laughter, almost in tears and said, "Wow, did you ever ask for that one! You can't be too mad with Tommy; after all, he is your son!"

With that the robot immediately walked over to Marsha and knocked her out of her chair.

"I must take every precaution not to get pregnant!" Sheri said to her friend. "But I thought your husband just had a vasectomy?" her friend responded. Sheri shrieked, "He did. That's why I have to take every precaution!!!"

A woman convinces her fiancé to wait until they get married to have sex. The night before the wedding his friends take him out and get him laid by every hooker in town. By the time he's done his penis so wrecked that he has to take two Popsicle sticks and wrap it up with adhesive tape.

The next day after the wedding, he's in the honeymoon suite and his wife comes out of the bathroom buck naked, points to her vagina and says, "Look dear, untouched by human hands!"

Thinking fast he unzips his fly, pulls it out and says, "Look dear, not even out of the crate!"

A man comes home early from work one day and sees his wife, on all fours scrubbing the floor, wearing nothing but a silk bathrobe. He sneaks up behind her, lifts up her robe, has his way with her and then smacks her in the head.

She turns around and says, "After you do something so nice, why would you hit me in the head like that?"

He snaps back, "That's for not looking to see who it was!"

The FBI had an opening for an assassin. After all the background checks, interviews and testing were done, there were 3 finalists; two men and a woman. For the final test, the FBI agents took one of the men to a metal door and handed him a gun. "We must know that you will follow your instructions no matter what the circumstances. Inside the room you'll find your wife sitting in a chair. Kill Her!"

The man said, "You can't be serious. I could never shoot my wife."

The agent said, "Then you're not right for this job. Take your wife and go home."

The second man was given the same instructions. He took the gun and went into the room. All was quiet for about 5 minutes. The man came out with tears in his eyes, "I tried, but I can't kill my wife."

The agent said, "You don't have what it takes. Take your wife and go home."

Finally, it was the woman's turn. She was told enter the room and kill her husband. She took the gun and went in. Shots were heard, one after another. There was screaming, crashing, and banging on the walls.

After a few minutes, all was quiet. The door opened slowly and there stood the woman, wiping the sweat from her brow. "The gun was loaded with blanks." she said. "So I had to beat him to death with the chair!"

A man annoys his wife at a dinner party. To get even, she tells him that last night she dreamt his penis was up for bid at a cock auction. Ignoring his glare, she goes on to tell him that huge cocks fetch $1000, large cocks snag $100 and small cocks only get $10.

"Great" he said, "how much did mine go for?" She says, "Oh, it didn't even get a bid."

So the next time they dined with friends he casually said, "Honey, you know what I dreamt about last night? It was really weird; we were at a vagina auction. Tight vaginas went for $10,000, loose ones for $100 and really huge, smelly, flappy ones for 10 cents." Intrigued, she asked much hers was sold for.

"Funny you ask" he says, "That's where we held the auction!"

When Ralph first noticed that his penis was growing larger and staying erect longer, he was almost as delighted as his wife. But after several weeks, his penis had grown to nearly twenty inches and Ralph became quite concerned. He was having problems dressing and even walking.

So he and his wife went to see a prominent urologist. After an initial examination, the doctor explained to the couple that, though rare Ralph's condition could be fixed through corrective surgery. "How long will Ralph be on crutches?" his wife asked anxiously.

"Crutches? Why would he need crutches?" responded the surprised doctor.

"Well," she said coldly, "you're gonna lengthen his legs, aren't you?"

A woman had been in a coma for months. Nurses were giving her a sponge bath. One of them was washing her private area and noticed that there was a slight response on the monitor when she touched her. They tried it again and sure enough there was a small, recognizable movement.

They went to her husband and explained what happened, "Crazy as this sounds, maybe a little oral sex will excite her and bring her out of the coma."

The husband was skeptical, but they assured that they'd close the curtains for privacy. The husband finally agreed and went into his wife's room. After a few minutes the woman's monitor flat lined, no pulse, no heart rate. The nurses ran into the room. "What happened?" they cried.

The husband said, "I'm not sure, I think she choked."

A guy in a ski mask burst into a sperm bank with a shotgun. "Open the safe!" he yells at the girl behind the counter.

She replies, "But sir, we don't have any money. This is a sperm bank."

"Don't argue, open the safe or I'll blow your head off!"

She nervously opened the safe. The guy says, "Take out one of the bottles and drink it!"

She exclaims, "But it's full of sperm!"

"Don't argue. Just drink it!" he says.

She takes the lid off and gulps it down. He yells, "Take out another bottle and drink it too."

She takes out another bottle of sperm and gulps it down.

Suddenly he pulls off his ski mask and to the girl's amazement; it's her husband. He says, "Now that's not so fucking difficult, is it?"

An elderly woman wanted to spice up her waning sex life so she went to Victoria's Secret and bought a pair of silk crotchless panties. That night, she stood in front of her husband and pointed to her new sexy undergarments, and seductively asked, "Dear, how about some of this?"

The old man growled, "No way dear; look what it did to your panties!"

Joe's wife loves singing so she decided to join the church choir. She would often practice while she was in the kitchen preparing dinner. Whenever she'd start in on a song, Joe would head outside to the porch. His wife, with hurt feelings, said, "What's the matter, Joe? Don't you like my singing?"

Joe replied, "Honey, I support your love for singing, but I just want to make sure the neighbors know I'm not beating you."

Luigi was dying and his wife, Michelle, was maintaining a candlelight vigil by his side. She held his fragile hand, tears running down her face. Her praying roused him from his slumber; he looked up and his pale lips began to move slightly. "Michelle, my darling…" he whispered.

"Hush my love," she said. "Rest, don't talk."

He was insistent. "Michelle," he said in his weakened voice, "I have something that I must confess."

"There's nothing to confess." replied the weeping Michelle, "Everything's all right, go to sleep."

"No, no my dear; I must die in peace. Michelle, I slept with your sister, your best friend, her best friend, and your mother!"

"I know sweetheart," whispered Michelle, "now just lay back and let the poison work."

A woman tells her husband, "I want breast implants!"

He says, "You know we can't afford it! Go grab a wad of toilet paper and rub it up and down in between your breasts."

"Will that really make them bigger?" she asked.

"Well, it worked on your ass...!"

Two guys are pushing their carts around Wal-Mart and they collide. The first guy says, "Sorry about that. I'm looking for my wife, and I guess I wasn't paying attention to where I was going."

The second guy says, "That's OK. I can't find my wife, either. I'm getting a little anxious."

"Well, maybe I can help you find her. What does she look like?"

"She's gorgeous, in her mid-twenties, tall, red hair, long legs, big chest, and she's wearing a red tank top and a black leather miniskirt. What does your wife look like?"

"The hell with mine, let's look for yours!!!"

A funeral is being held for a woman who has just passed away. At the end of the service, the pallbearers are carrying the casket out when they accidentally bump into a wall, jarring the casket. They hear a faint moan. They open the casket and find that the woman is actually alive! She lives for ten more years, and then dies.

Once again, a ceremony is held, and at the end of it, the pallbearers are again carrying out the casket. As they carry the casket towards the door, the husband cries out, "Watch that wall!"

A couple had a dog that constantly snored. Annoyed because she can't sleep, the wife goes to the vet for help. He tells her to tie a ribbon around the dog's testicles and he'll stop snoring.

A few minutes after going to bed, the dog begins snoring as usual and the wife tosses and turns, unable to sleep. So she goes to the closet and grabs a piece of red ribbon & ties it carefully around the dog's testicles. Sure enough, the dog stops snoring! She is amazed! Later that night, her husband returns home drunk. He climbs into bed, passes out, and begins snoring loudly. She thinks maybe the ribbon might work on him. So she goes to the closet again, grabs a piece of blue ribbon and ties it around his testicles. Amazingly, it also worked on him!

The woman slept soundly but her husband woke from his drunken stupor and stumbled into the bathroom. Standing in front of the toilet, he glanced in the mirror and saw that there was a blue ribbon wrapped around his privates. Very confused, he walked back into the bedroom where he also noticed that there was a red ribbon attached to his dog's testicles.

He shakes his head and says, "I don't know what we did last night, boy. But, by God, we took first and second place!"

A couple is spending their 20th anniversary in the very same bed in the very same hotel room. The wife says, "Harry, what were you thinking about 20 years ago on this very night?"

"I was thinking that I'd like to fuck your brains out." he said.

"Well, what are you thinking now?" she asked.

He smiled a sheepish grin and said, "I think I did!"

A college professor is lying in bed reading while his wife sleeps. Every few minutes, he reaches over and tickles her between the legs. After several times she sat up and screamed, "Will you stop that?! You're teasing me!"

He replied, "I'm not teasing you. I'm just wetting my fingers so I can turn the page!"

A woman walks up to the prescription counter at the pharmacy and says, "I need some cyanide or some chemical like it to kill my husband!"

"Ma'am, you can't just walk in here and order chemicals like that and it's against the law to kill your husband." he answers.

She rustles around in her purse and produces a manila folder and pulls out something and hands it to the pharmacist. It's a photo of her husband having sex with the pharmacist's wife.

The pharmacist replies, "Oh, I didn't realize you had a prescription!"

Rick repeatedly refused his friend Al's offer of free tickets to sporting events, always saying, "I can't, Cotter is playing tonight."

Al finally asked, "Who the hell is this Cotter guy anyway?"

Rick said, "He plays the sax in a jazz band in a pub across town."

Al responded, "So what?"

"So, when he plays..." Rick explained, "I fuck his wife!"

A couple was married for 20 years and every time they

made love, the husband still always insisted on shutting off the light. The wife felt this was ridiculous so she figured she would break him out of this crazy habit. One night, while they were in the middle of a wild, screaming, romantic session, she turned on the lights. She looked down and saw he was holding a battery-operated vibrator!

She went completely ballistic, screaming, "You impotent piece of shit! How could you be lying to me all of these years? You better explain yourself!"

He looked her straight in the eyes and calmly said, "I'll explain the toy, you explain the kids!"

An old man had worked his whole life in a pickle factory. One day he came home and told his wife that he got fired. She screamed, "You gave them 20 years of devoted service! Why did they fire you?"

"You see," he explained, "for twenty years I've wanted to stick my pecker in the pickle-slicer and today I finally did it!"

She ran over and pulled his pants down to see what damage had been done. "You look okay," she said with a sigh of relief.

"So what happened to the pickle-slicer?"

"Well," he said with hesitation, "they fired her, too."

A married couple was in the living room talking and the subject of a "Living Will" came up. The husband said, "I never want to live in a vegetative state, dependent on some machine and fluids from a bottle. If I ever come to that just pull the plug."

So she got up, unplugged the TV, and poured out his beer.

A couple in their 60's were celebrating their 40th wedding

anniversary. On their special day a fairy came to them and said that because they had been such a devoted couple she would grant each of them a special wish. The wife wished for a trip around the world with her husband. Whoosh! Immediately, she had airline and cruise tickets in her hands. The man wished for a female companion 30 years younger. Whoosh! Immediately, he turned ninety!

For her wedding, Camilla Parker Bowles bought brand-new shoes, which grew increasingly tighter as the big day went on. That evening, when the festivities were finally over, the newly-weds retired to their quarters in Buckingham Palace. Flopping on the king-size bed, Camilla cooed, "Charles, darling, please remove my shoes. My feet are killing me!"

So Charles got down on his knees and attacked Camilla's right shoe with vigor, but it wouldn't budge. "Harder!" she yelled. "Harder!"

"I'm trying, darling!" Charles roared. "But it's just so bloody tight!"

She pled, "Come on luv; give it all you've got!" When the stubborn shoe finally came off Charles let out a big groan and Camilla exclaimed, "Oh, God that feels sooo good!"

Lying in the royal bedroom next door, Queen Elizabeth said to her husband, Prince Phillip, "See, dear? I told you with a face like that, she was still a virgin!"

Meanwhile, as Charles persistently tried to remove Camilla's other shoe, he cried, "Oh, God, darling! This one's even tighter!"

Prince Phillip said proudly, "That's my boy. Once a Navy man, always a Navy man!"

A woman got a terrible headache and told her husband to

go to a swanky Halloween Party alone. She took an aspirin and went to bed, so he took his costume and left. She slept soundly for an hour and awakened without pain and, as it was still early, decided to go to the party.

Her husband didn't know what her costume was. She thought she'd have some fun by watching him to see how he acts when she wasn't with him. She joined the party and soon spotted him cavorting around the dance floor, dancing with every chick he could, and copping a feel here and there. She sidled up to him and, being a rather seductive babe herself, he was all over her.

She let him go as far as he wished, naturally, since he was her husband. Finally, he whispered a little proposition in her ear and she agreed, so off they went into the bathroom and had a little quickie. Just before unmasking at midnight, she slipped away and went home; eagerly awaiting his excuse for his behavior. When he came in, she asked how his evening was.

He said, "Oh, the same old thing. You know, I never have a good time when you're not there."

Then she asked, "Did you dance much?" He replied, "I'll tell you, I never even danced once. When I got there I me, Pete, Bill, and Paul just played poker in the back room all evening. But you're not going to believe what happened to the guy I loaned my costume to!!!"

The Husband Store

A store that sells husbands has just recently opened in New York City. At the entrance is a description of how the store operates: 1) You may visit the store only ONCE! 2) There are six floors and the men's attributes increase at each one. 3) You may choose any man from a particular floor, or you may choose to go up a floor, but you cannot go back down a floor except to exit the building!

The first customer of the day enters the store to go shopping for a husband. The sign on the 1st floor door reads: "These men have jobs and love the Lord." She continues up.

The sign on the 2nd floor reads: "These men have jobs, love the Lord, and love kids." Nope.

The 3rd floor sign reads: "These men have jobs, love the Lord, love kids, and are extremely good looking." She is intrigued but feels compelled to keep going.

She goes to the fourth floor where the sign reads: "These men are drop-dead gorgeous, have jobs, love the Lord, love kids, AND help with the housework." "Oh, mercy me!" she exclaims, "I can hardly stand it!"

Still, she heads up to the fifth floor: "These men are drop-dead gorgeous, amazing in bed, have very high paying jobs, love the Lord, love kids, help with the housework, and are extremely romantic."

She can't imagine how it could possibly get any better than this and she is tempted to stay. But her curiosity and innate desire for perfection get the best of her and she excitedly marches up to the sixth floor: "You are visitor 4,363,012. There are NO MEN on this floor. This floor exists solely as proof that women are impossible to please. Thank you for shopping at the Husband Store. Watch your step as you exit the building, and have a nice day!

3

Sex

I've never met another human being that doesn't love sex. I've met plenty of people are sick of sex with their current partner but, aside from that, I think we can all agree that sex is an activity enjoyed by everyone. That's probably why jokes on this subject have a universal appeal.

Comedians refer to these as "dick jokes" (no explanation should be necessary) and always have a bag full at the ready in case they find themselves in a jam. A good "dick joke" will win the crowd back almost every single time. We'd rather not have to resort to them but it's comforting to have a good back up plan should all else fail. Besides, they're fun as hell to tell!

A Bagful of Dick Jokes

Two sperm are swimming along. One sperm turns to the other and says, "Hey man, I'm exhausted! When the hell are we going to get to the uterus?" The other sperm laughs, "Uterus? We haven't even made it passed the esophagus!!!"

A woman gets stranded on a dessert island with 3 guys. After a week, she feels so guilty about what she's been doing with them she kills herself. A week later, the guys feel so guilty about what they've been doing with her they decide to bury her. One week after that, they feel so guilty about what they've been doing with each other; they dig her back up...

The owner of an adult pleasure spa was showing a new arrival around. "You'll love it here; especially the barrel behind the rest room. Whenever you feel the need, just stick your dick in the hole for the most amazing blowjob you've ever had in your entire life."

The next day, he ran into the owner, "This place is great! I'm going to use that barrel everyday!"

"Well, everyday but Monday," said the owner. The guy asked, "Why not Monday?"

The owner smiled, "That's your day in the barrel!"

Nick, strolling down the boardwalk in Atlantic City, ran into a hooker and asked, "How much?" "$20" she says. So he takes her under the pier and nails her. The next day he sees the same hooker and takes her back under the pier. But this time, when he's in the middle of screwing her, she let's out two huge farts. When they get done and he gives her $25.

She says, "What the extra $5 for?"

Nick says, "That's for blowing the sand off my balls!"

Madam Bovey ran a successful whorehouse but, times were getting tough and she needed some extra money. One day she decided to add another bedroom by putting a partition between the reception area and the office. So she called a carpenter to come in and put up the new wall. "Okay Madam, that'll be $1500."

She takes him by the hand, leads him into the new bedroom, sits him in a chair, takes off her clothes, rubs her tits up against him and seductively says, "Ya' know, I'm a little short on cash so, maybe we can take it out in trade?"

He smiles as he puts a finger in her ass and his thumb in her pussy and says, "Lady, give me my $1500 bucks or I'm gonna rip out this partition!"

On his eighteenth birthday, Billy says, "Hey Dad, can I have twenty dollars for a blowjob?" His Dad replies, "I don't know son, are you any good?"

Superman just finished saving the universe and was out flying around to relax. As he was zipping over Central Park, he saw Wonder Woman lying alone on the grass, naked, legs spread... He didn't want to miss this opportunity but he also didn't want to damage their friendship. So he decided to use his super power and fly in & out without her knowing whom it was. He flew down and "BAM", nailed her and quickly flew away. She sprang up, "What the hell was that?"

The Invisible Man says, "I don't know but my ass is killing me!"

Dr. Bob had slept with one of his patients and felt guilty all day long. No matter how much he tried to forget about it, he couldn't. His guilt was overwhelming. But every once in a while he'd hear a reassuring voice that said, "Bob, don't worry about it. You aren't the first doctor to sleep with one of their patients, and you won't be the last. And you're single. Let it go."

But invariably another voice would bring him back to reality: "Bob, you're a veterinarian!"

Cotter is drowning his sorrows at the bar when a beautiful young lady takes a seat next to him. "I'm so depressed" she says, "My husband threw me out because I was way too kinky for him." Cotter laments, "That's weird because my wife also just dumped me for being too kinky." Then he says, "I've got an idea; because we're both so kinky, maybe you and I should get together?"

"Hey yeah, that's a great idea!" she replies. "Let's go back to my place."

So they go to her apartment. She says, "Make yourself at home while I go slip into something less comfortable, if you know what I mean." He smiles as she walks into her bedroom. She returns wearing spiked heels, leather chaps, a whip, and handcuffs, but he's not there. Instead, she finds a note reading; "I shit in your purse, fucked your dog, and shoved your goldfish up my ass... I'm outta' here!"

A young couple was about to make love when suddenly a bumblebee flew in the window and right into her snatch. She screamed, "Oh God help, there's a bee in my vagina!" The husband rushed her to the doctor and explained the situation. The doctor thought for a moment, "Hmm, tricky situation, but I do have a solution if you'd permit." The husband nodded.

The doctor continued, "Okay, I'll rub honey on the tip of my penis and insert it into her vagina. When I feel the bee getting closer to the tip, I'll withdraw the penis and the bee will follow it out." His wife plead, "Yes, whatever, please just get it out!" The husband reluctantly gave his approval.

So the doctor coated his penis with honey and inserted it into her. After a few gentle strokes, he said, "I don't think the bee has noticed the honey yet. Perhaps I should go a bit deeper." So the doctor went deeper and deeper. After a while the doctor began shafting her very hard. She began quivering with excitement, moaning and groaning. The doctor caressed her breasts with one hand then started spanking himself with his free hand while grunting and moaning loudly.

At this point, the husband became very annoyed, "What the hell do you think you're doing?"

The doctor moaned, "Change of plan. I'm gonna drown the bastard!"

A researcher for the Vaseline Company called a young mother one night. "Ma'am, I'm conducting a survey of our product, Vaseline. While it has many uses, such as greasing a bike chain, a door hinge, or chapped lips, many people claim they use it to enhance sexual intercourse. Do you use our product in any of these ways?"

The young mother replied, "Well, my husband and I only use it when we're having sex."

"Would you mind telling me how you use our product?" he asked.

"Sure, we put it on the doorknob to keep the kids out!"

A mother was walking down the hall when she heard a humming sound coming from her daughter's room. As she opened the door, she found her naked, sprawled out on the bed, using a vibrator. "What the hell are you doing?"

The daughter replied, "Look, I'm 35, single, and still living with my parents. This vibrator is probably the closest I'll ever get to a husband!"

Later that week, her father was in the kitchen and heard a humming sound coming from the basement. He went downstairs and found his daughter lying buck-naked on the couch, legs behind her head, using a vibrator. "My Lord, what the hell are you doing?" he asked.

She explained, "I'm 35, single, still living with my parents... this is the closest I'll ever get to a husband."

A few days later, the mother heard the familiar humming noise coming from the den. Upon entering, she found her husband on the sofa, drinking a beer, watching TV with the vibrator buzzing away beside him. "What on earth are you doing?" she cried.

He replied, "Be quiet, I'm trying to watch the game with my son-in-law!"

A girl asks her new boyfriend to have dinner with her parents. Since this is such a big event, she tells him that after dinner she wants to have sex with him for the first time. The boy is ecstatic, but has never had sex before, so he goes to the pharmacy to get some condoms. The pharmacist talks to the boy for an hour, telling him all about condoms and sex. Finally, the pharmacist asks him if he'd like to buy a 3-pack, 10-pack or family pack.

The boy insists on the family pack because he thinks he will be rather busy, it being his first time and all. That night he shows up at her door. "Oh, I'm so excited for you to meet my parents! Come on in!" She takes him to the dinner table where her parents are seated. The boy quickly offers to say grace and bows his head. A minute passes and he's still deep in prayer, head down. 10 minutes pass, still no movement. Finally, after

20 minutes, the girl whispers, "I had no idea you were this religious."

The boy whispers back, "I had no idea your father was a pharmacist!"

Why is it when a man talks dirty to a woman its "sexual harassment" but when a woman talks dirty to man its $3.99 a minute?

Dick Joke Q&A

Q: Why is the head of the penis bigger than the shaft?
A: So your hand doesn't fly off and smack you in the face!

Q: What's the difference between pink & purple?
A: Your grip.

Q: What's the difference between "Oooh" and "Ahhh"?
A: Three inches.

Q: What do you say to a woman with no arms or legs?
A: "Hey, nice tits!"

Q: What's the difference between screwing a woman with arms and one without arms?
A: When screwing a woman without arms and it pops out, you have to put it back in...

Q: How can you tell when an auto mechanic has just had sex?
A: One of his fingers is clean.

Q: What's the difference between a microwave and anal sex?
A: A microwave won't brown your meat.

Q: What's the difference between mayonnaise & semen?
A: Mayonnaise doesn't hit the back of a girl's throat at thirty miles an hour.

Q: How is pubic hair like parsley?
A: You push it to the side before you start eating.

My Dick Is So Big...

Does size really matter? Hell yeah it does, especially when we're talking about dick jokes. I've heard rumors that comedian Drew Carey was the first to pioneer the "My dick is so big..." franchise. It wouldn't surprise me given how damn funny he is but I can't back that up. I don't know the exact origin of the jokes below. All I can tell you is that my dick is so big... during WWII Ann Frank hid in it!

My dick is so big there's still snow on it in the summertime.

My dick is so big it won't return Spielberg's calls.

My dick is so big it graduated a year ahead of me from high school.

My dick is so big it has an elevator and a lobby.

SEX

My dick is so big, clowns climb out of it when I cum.

My dick is so big I'm already fucking a girl tomorrow.

My dick is so big I entered it in a big-dick contest and it came in first, second, and third.

My dick is so big ships use it to find their way into the harbor.

My dick is so big there was once a movie called Godzilla vs. My Dick.

My dick is so big King Kong is going to crawl up it in the next remake.

My dick is so big no matter where I go; my dick always gets there first.

My dick is so big I use the Eiffel Tower as a French tickler.

My dick is so big when it rains the head of my dick doesn't get wet.

My dick is so big a homeless family lives underneath it.

My dick is so big they use the bullet train to test my condoms.

My dick is so big I use a hula hoop as a cock ring.

My dick is so big we use it at parties as a limbo pole.

My dick is so big I can fuck an elevator shaft.

My dick is so big Stephen Hawking has a theory about it.

My dick is so big it warps the space-dick continuum.

My dick is so big my first orgasm caused the Big Bang.

My dick is so big every time I get hard I cause a solar eclipse.

My dick is so big the inside of my dick contains billions and billions of stars.

My dick is so big interplanetary distances are measured in light years and my dick years.

My dick is so big that we're all a part of it and it's all a part of us.

My dick is so big that it has its own dick. And even my dick's dick is bigger than your dick.

My dick is so big it doesn't have veins, it has pipes.

My dick is so big I have to check it as luggage when I fly.

My dick is so big it has a personal trainer.

My dick is so big that right now it's in the other room fixing us drinks.

My dick is so big it has a retractable dome.

My dick is so big it has stairs up the center like the Statue of Liberty.

My dick is so big there's a sneaker named "Air My Dick."

My dick is so big it's against the law to fuck me without protective headgear.

My dick is so big it violates seventeen zoning laws.

My dick is so big movie theaters now serve popcorn in small, medium, large, and My Dick.

My dick is so big I was once in Ohio and got a blow job in Tennessee.

My dick is so big Las Vegas casinos fly it into town for free.

My dick is so big the Carnegie Deli named a sandwich after it. Actually, two sandwiches.

My dick is so big the city was going to build a statue of it but they ran out of cement.

My dick is so big it plays golf with the president.

My dick is so big it charges money for its autograph.

My dick is so big it has an agent; my dick's people will call your people. Let's do lunch with my dick.

My dick is so big when I was in a porno they had to release it on a 4 disc DVD box set.

My dick is so big it thinks the Grand Canyon is a virgin.

My dick is so big it bought Microsoft from petty cash.

My dick is so big I run three-legged races by myself.

My dick is so big when I fall down, I fuck everyone in China.

My dick is so big that I look like its dick in front of it.

My dick is so big compasses do not function properly around it.

My dick is so big the Pope has blessed it.

My dick is so big premature ejaculation takes ninety minutes.

My dick is so big it's in a boy band with four other big dicks.

My dick is so big I use it to smuggle illegal immigrants across the border.

My dick is so big if I didn't sleep on my side, planes would crash into it at night.

My dick is so big Frodo carried the Ring to it.

My dick is so big Osama bin Laden tried to fly a 747 into it.

SEX

My dick is so big Magellan only sailed halfway around it.

My dick is so big Columbus discovered it and thought it was India.

My dick is so big it was mistakenly claimed for Spain by de Portola in 1629.

My dick is so big my parents had to get a building permit to have me circumcised.

My dick is so big it wears longer pants than I do.

My dick is so big it hit .370 in the minors before it hurt its knee.

My dick is so big Henry Aaron used it to hit his 750th home run.

My dick is so big it was almost drafted by the NY Yankees, but George Steinbrenner didn't want a bigger dick than he was on the team.

My dick is so big that when it's Eastern Standard Time at the tip, it's Central Mountain Time at my balls.

My dick is so big it has its own time zone - central dick time.

My dick is so big I went to The Viper Room and my dick got right in. I had to stand and argue with the doorman.

My dick is so big Google Maps had to move satellites higher into orbit just to photograph it.

My dick is so big it was overthrown by a military coup. It's now known as the People's Republic of My Dick.

My dick is so big Rolling Stone calls it "The Fifth Beatle."

My dick is so big there was a band called Earth, Wind and My Dick.

My dick is so big it hosted Saturday Night Live - twice!

My dick is so big it costs a fortune to heat.

My dick is so big it has a gift shop. People buy bumper stickers that say they visited My Dick.

My dick is so big Hurricane Katrina gave me a blowjob.

My dick is so big I have to buy it its own airline seat.

My dick is so big it could have invaded Iraq all by itself.

My dick is so big it has its own national anthem.

My dick is so big it beat up the class bully in high school.

My dick is so big it's listed on the New York Stock Exchange.

My dick is so big the sperm bank opened a branch office just for it.

SEX

My dick is so big I have to pay property taxes on it.

My dick is so big the Titanic ran into it and sank.

My dick is so big scientists think it killed off the dinosaurs.

My dick is so big you can get lost on it and wander for days.

My dick is so big you can see your house from it.

My dick is so big it has a tollbooth at both ends.

My dick is so big there's an observatory on it.

My dick is so big it has a really good beach and several ok ones.

My dick is so big there are isolated tribes living on remote areas of it.

My dick is so big the Amazon detours around it.

My dick is so big my balls have never seen the sky.

My dick is so big I have to establish a base camp before sex.

My dick is so big my grandmother knits it sweaters.

My dick is so big it has its own zip code.

My dick is so big it can be used as a flotation device in the unlikely event of a water landing.

My dick is so big that I got it stuck in my zipper and didn't scream until I felt it two days later.

My dick is so big the Patriots acquired it to play football-next year; it'll be the entire front line.

My dick is so big that there're currently a bunch of biologists filming a documentary on its untamed inhabitants.

My dick can look directly into a second-story window, flat-footed.

My dick is so big that pranksters show up at night; stomping all over it making fake crop circles.

My dick is so big it bullies all the smaller dicks out of their lunch money.

My dick is so big that its flight is impossible without the aid of rising thermal updrafts.

My dick is so big that Hannibal tried to ride it across the Himalayas.

My dick is so big visitors at the zoo buy bags of peanuts to stuff up it.

My dick is so big that just keeping it painted is an unending chore.

My dick is so big lots of people think we're brothers.

My dick is so big the DMV is requiring me to obtain a Class B license.

My dick is so big it changed its name to an unpronounceable symbol formerly known as Dick.

My dick is so big early mapmakers depicted it as a sea monster.

My dick is so big it came to America on the Nina, the Pinta and the Santa Maria.

My dick is so big it could've fed the entire Donner Party-for two winters!

My dick is so big it takes two days and a good pack mule to get up to the tip.

My dick requires backcountry permits for all overnight hikes.

My dick is so big it has to downshift on steep grades.

My dick is so big smaller dicks experience severe turbulence from my dick's wingtip vortices.

My dick is so big it has P-Diddy on speed dial.

My dick is so big all the smaller dicks roll over, showing their bellies in submission.

My dick is so big it stubbornly drives around lost for hours and never stops to ask for directions.

My dick is so big it takes 1 ½ miles to make a 90 degree turn.

My dick and Las Vegas, NV create the exact same size carbon footprint.

My dick is so big it has a private helipad.

My dick is so big I have to bus in day laborers just to fidget with my balls.

My dick is so big it has Yosemite Sam mud flaps.

My dick is so big the bumper sticker on back warns motorists not to drive in its blind spot.

My dick is so big the Eskimos have over 40 unique words that mean "my dick."

My dick is so big I'm already banging my next girlfriend's best friend.

My dick is so big if you climbed to the tip, you could see your house from there.

My dick is so big that Verizon's leasing space at the tip for a cell phone tower.

My dick is so big it has a four-lane bowling alley.

My dick is so big I gotta use binoculars to make sure that ain't no man down there sucking it.

My dick is so big you'd better just get the Cliff's Notes version.

My dick is so big visitors are delighted with its scenic beauty as well as the deluxe accommodations, snack bar and pro-shop.

My dick is so big penthouse guests have reported there's a noticeable sway on windy days.

My dick is recommended by four out of five dentists, and their patients who chew my dick.

My dick is so big it spoils every single Christmas; waking up early and opening all the presents under the tree.

My dick is so big it's become aloof; maintaining just a nodding acquaintance with my balls and won't even speak to my asshole anymore.

My dick is so big novice divers must pressure-equalize their ears several times on the way down.

My dick is so big it can sit in the front row at Sea World and Shamu doesn't dare splash it.

My dick is so big it is slated to host the 2016 Summer Olympics.

My dick is so big they won't let it ride any of the coasters at Six Flags.

My dick is so big it'll be presenting a fireworks extravaganza after the show.

My dick is so big rising fuel costs have forced it to cancel its summer travel plans.

My dick is so big it periodically sheds its skin. I got enough last month to make a pair of motorcycle boots, three wallets and a circus tent.

My dick is so big it must signal with three long horn blasts before making sternway.

My dick is so big it blows out the candles no matter whose birthday it is.

My dick is so big they had to use bolt cutters for my vasectomy.

My dick is so big my bed is equipped with airbags.

My dick is so big I have to set up orange traffic cones when I take a piss outside.

My dick is so big I have to wear a back brace when I masturbate.

My dick is so big sometimes it jerks me off.

My dick is so big my urologist has to rent a forklift for my annual prostate exam.

My dick is so big its part of the government bailout plan.

My dick is so big the Chief of Staff holds briefings about it.

My dick is so big even after 101 jokes, it's still pretty funny.

4

Old Age

Face it: Unless you prematurely buy the farm from an untimely heart attack after mixing cocaine, vodka, and Viagra at an S&M orgy hosted by Parris Hilton and the Olsen twins, you are going to be old someday. So go right ahead and make fun of old people all you want, just keep in mind this will be you too, my friend – and much sooner than you expect! Now where in tarnation did I leave my damn reading glasses...?

Confucius Say: Best way to get a man to do something is to suggest he's too old for it.

Confucius Say: He's so old... he remembers when the Dead Sea was only sick.

Q: What do you call a 90 year old man who can still masturbate?
A: Miracle Whip.

Q. Back in the old days, when Grandpa put horseradish on his head, what was he trying to do?
A. Get it in his mouth.

Q: What's the best part about Alzheimer's Disease?
A: You can hide your own Easter Eggs.

An 80-year-old man goes to the doctor, the doctor says, "You've got Alzheimer's Disease and Cancer." The old man says, "Well, at least I don't have cancer!"

A couple married for 25 years were making love for hours and neither had climaxed. Finally, the husband looked down and asked, "What's the matter can't think of anyone else either?

An old man was reluctantly put in a nursing home by his son. His first morning there he wakes up with a hard on. Out of nowhere, a beautiful young nurse walks in, kneels down, and blows him without saying a word. Later, he gets on the phone, "Son, I love this place. Thank you for sending me here!" He replies, "Wow, you sound really happy. What happened?" He said, "You won't believe it; I woke up with an erection and this gorgeous nurse came in and just blew me." The son says, "Well congratulations! I knew you'd adjust to being there."
Later, the old man is walking down the hall and slips, falls, and can't get up. Suddenly, this redneck orderly comes up behind him, rips his pants off, and fucks him up the ass, leaving him lying there in a heap. The old man crawls to the phone and calls his son, "Kid, you gotta get me out of here. This place is nuts!" He replies, "What happened? I thought you were happy?" He explained, "I just tripped & fell and this big orderly tore my pants off and boned me up the ass."

"Well you know Pop; you got a blowjob this morning. You'll have to take the good with the bad."

The old man exclaims, "Son, you don't understand; I only get a hard on once every few months! I fall down at least three, four times a day!"

A young punk rocker with red & purple-feathered hair, safety pin through the nose, tattoos all over his body, gets on a bus and sits down next to an old guy who keeps staring at him. Finally, the punk says, "What're you lookin' at old man? Didn't you ever do anything crazy when you were a kid?" The old man replies, "Yup, I once fucked a parrot. I thought you might be my son!"

An elderly couple is visiting the doctor's office. The doctor says to the old man, "I'll need a urine sample, a feces sample, and a blood sample." The old man, hard of hearing, says, "What?" So the doctor says it again, a little louder. Once again the old man says, "What?"

The doctor finally yells, "I need a sample of urine, feces, and blood!" Still no response from the old man. Annoyed, the woman turns to her husband, "He said he needs a pair of your underwear!"

An elderly man lay dying in his bed. As death approached, he suddenly smelled the aroma of his favorite chocolate chip cookies wafting up the stairs. He gathered his remaining strength and lifted himself from the bed. Gripping the wall, he made his way out of the room and forced himself down the stairs. With labored breath, he leaned against the doorframe and gazed into the kitchen. There, spread out on the table was his favorite chocolate chip cookies. Was it heaven or the final act of love from his devoted wife, making sure that he left this world a happy man?

With one last great effort, he threw himself toward the table, landing on his knees. His lips parted; the wondrous smell of the cookies slowly bringing him back to life. His hand weakly reached for a cookie at the edge of the table, when his wife suddenly smacked it with a spatula. "Stay out of those," she said, "they're for the funeral."

Two elderly sisters, Margaret and Eleanor, had been close for many decades, sharing all kinds of activities and adventures. Lately, their activities had been limited to meeting a few times a week to play cards. One day, in the middle of a Bridge game, Margaret looked at Eleanor and said, "Now don't get mad at me; I know you're my sister but I just can't think of your name! I've thought and thought, and for the life of me, I can't remember. Please tell me your name."

Eleanor sat and glared at her for a few minutes then sheepishly replied, "How soon do you need to know?"

Two old sisters, Hazel and Eleanor, were out driving, barely able to see over the dashboard. Cruising along, they came to an intersection, the light was red but Hazel sped right through. Eleanor thought to herself, "Gee, I must be losing my mind, that light looked red to me."

Moments later, they came to another red light and again, Hazel blew right threw it. Eleanor thought, "I really must be losing it. I could've sworn that light was red. I should pay closer attention.

At the next intersection, sure enough, the light was red and Hazel zipped passed it. Eleanor turned to her, "Hazel, you just ran three lights in a row. You could have killed us!!!"

Hazel said, "Oh shit! Am I driving?"

Herman, 87, was driving down the freeway when his phone rang. It was his wife urgently warning, "Honey, I just heard on the news there's a car going the wrong way on the freeway. Be careful!"

"Shoot," said Herman, "It's not just one car. It's hundreds of them!"

A guy visits his grandmother and while they're chatting, he eats an entire bowl of peanuts from the coffee table. Leaving he said, "Thanks Grammy. Those peanuts were delicious!"

She says, "Yeah, ever since I lost my dentures I can only suck the chocolate off 'em."

Harold, age 95, lives in a senior citizen home. Every night after dinner, he goes to a secluded garden behind the center to sit and ponder his long life. One evening, Hazel, age 87, wanders into the garden. They begin to chat, and before they know it, several hours have passed. After a short lull in their conversation, he says to Hazel, "Do you know what I miss most of all? I miss sex." She exclaims, "Why you old fart, you couldn't get it up if I held a gun to your head!" "I know," Harold says, "but it would be nice if a woman could just hold it for a while." "Well, I can oblige," says Hazel, who unzips his trousers, removes his penis and proceeds to hold it.

Afterward, they agree to meet secretly each night in the garden where they would sit and talk and Hazel would hold Harold's manhood. Then, one night, Harold didn't show up at their usual meeting place. Alarmed, she went to find Harold to make sure he was okay. After a while she found him sitting by the pool with Ethel, who was holding his penis in her old hand. Furious, Hazel yelled, "You two-timing creep! What does Ethel have that I don't have?"

Old Harold smiled happily and replied, "Parkinson's."

Two old guys, 80 and 87, were sitting on their usual park bench one morning. The 87 yr old had just finished his morning jog and wasn't even short of breath. The 80 yr old was amazed at his friend's stamina and asked what he did to have so much energy. The 87 yr old said, "Well, I eat rye bread every day. It keeps your energy level high and you'll have great stamina with the ladies."

On the way home, the 80 yr old man stopped off at the bakery. As he was looking around, the lady asked if he needed any help. He said, "Yes, I'd like five loaves of Rye bread." She said, "My goodness, five loaves? By the time you get to the 5th loaf, it'll be hard."

He replied, "I can't believe it, everybody knows about this shit but me!"

A lonely old widow decided that it was time to get married again so she put an ad in the local paper that read: "HUSBAND WANTED: must be in my age group, must not run around on me, must not beat me, and must be good in bed! All applicants please apply in person."

The next day, she heard the doorbell. Much to her dismay, she opened the door to see a grey-haired gentleman sitting in a wheelchair. He had no arms or legs. The old woman, visibly disappointed said, "You're not really asking me to consider you, are you? You have no legs!"

The old man just flashed a smile, "Therefore my good lady, I cannot run around on you!"

Somewhat aghast she snorted, "But sir, you do not have any arms either!"

Again, he smiled and gave a wink, "Therefore my good lady, I can never beat you!"

She raised an eyebrow and asked intently, "Well, are you at least good in bed?"

The old man leaned back, grinning ear-to-ear, and said, "Rang the doorbell didn't I?"

An old retired sailor puts on his old uniform and heads to the docks once more for old times sake. He engages a prostitute and takes her up to a room. He's giving it to her as best as he can, but still needing some reassurance so he asks, "How'm I doin'?"

"Well, old sailor," she replies, "You're doing about three knots."

"Three knots? What's that mean?"

She says, "You're not hard, you're not in, and you're not getting your money back!"

An old man was sitting on a park bench sobbing. A young guy walked up to him and asked "What's wrong?" The old man replied, "I am married to a gorgeous, sexy 21 year old blonde who gives me two blowjobs a day and all the sex I could ever want!" The young guy was puzzled, "It sounds to me like you have got it made! I don't see what the problem can be?"

The old man replied, "I can't remember where I live!"

A Florida couple, well into their 80s, goes to a sex therapist's office. The doctor asks, "What can I do for you?" The man says, "Will you watch us have sexual intercourse?" The doctor is puzzled, but is so amazed that such an elderly couple is asking for sexual advice that he agrees. When the couple finishes, the doctor says, "There's absolutely nothing wrong with the way you have intercourse." He thanks them for coming, charges them $50 and says goodbye.

The next week, however, the couple returns and asks the sex therapist to watch again. The sex therapist is a bit puzzled, but agrees. This happens several weeks in a row. The couple makes an appointment, have intercourse with no problems, pay the doctor, then leave.

Finally, after 5 or 6 weeks of this routine, the doctor says, "I'm sorry, but I have to ask; just what are you trying to find out?" The old man says, "We're not trying to find out anything. She's married and we can't go to her house. I'm married and we can't go to my house. The Holiday Inn charges $98. The Hilton charges $139. We do it here for $50, and I get $43 back from Medicare!"

An elderly couple was having problems remembering things so they went to the doctor for a checkup. He tells them they're physically okay, but they might want to start writing things down to help them remember. Later that night while watching TV, the old man gets up from his chair. His wife asked where he was going. "To the kitchen." he replies.

"Will you get me a bowl of ice cream?"

"Sure."

"Don't you think you should write it down so you can remember it?"

"No, I can remember it."

"I'd like some strawberries on top, too. You really should write it down in case you forget."

"I can remember that! You want a bowl of ice cream with strawberries."

"I'd also like whipped cream. I'm certain you'll forget that, so please write it down!"

"I don't need to write it down! I can remember! Ice cream with strawberries and whipped cream! I got it, for cryin' out loud!"

He grumbles into the kitchen. After about 20 minutes he returns and hands his wife a plate of bacon and eggs. She looks down at the plate and says, "Where's my toast?"

Arthur is 90 years old. He's played golf every day since his retirement 25 years ago. One day he arrived home looking downcast. "That's it" he tells his wife. "I'm giving up golf. My eyesight has gotten so bad that once I hit the ball I can't see where it goes." His wife sympathizes, "Why don't you take my brother Tom with you and give it one more try?"

"That's no good," sighs Arthur, "Tom is a hundred and three. He can't help."

She replies, "He may be a hundred and three but his eyesight is perfect." So the next day Arthur heads off to the golf course with his brother-in-law. He tees up, takes an almighty swing and squints down the fairway. He turns to Tom, "Did you see the ball?"

"Of course I did!" replied Tom. "I have perfect eyesight."

"Well, where did it go?"

Tom laments, "I don't remember!"

An elderly gentleman went to the local drug store and asked the pharmacist for Viagra. The pharmacist said, "That's no problem. How many do you want?" The man answered, "Just a few, maybe 4, but cut each one in 4 pieces." The pharmacist said, "That won't do you any good."

The elderly gentleman said, "That's all right, I don't need them for sex anymore. I'm 80 years old. I just want it to stick out far enough so I don't pee on my shoes!"

Dorothy and Edna are sitting on the front porch of the Senior Citizens home. Dorothy says, "That nice George Johnson asked me out for a date. I know you went out with him last week, and I wanted to talk with you about him before I gave him an answer."

Edna says, "Well, I'll tell you; he showed up at my door promptly at 7, dressed like a gentleman in a fine suit, and he brought me such beautiful flowers! He took me outside, and what's waiting? A shiny black limousine with a uniformed chauffeur and all! Then he took me out for dinner, and such a marvelous dinner it was! Lobster, champagne, anything I wanted. After dinner we had drinks then went to see a show. Let me tell you, Dorothy, I was having the time of my life! So then, after all that, we came back to my apartment and he turned into an ANIMAL! He completely tore off my dress, and had his way with me two times!"

Dorothy clutches her chest, "My goodness! So you're saying I shouldn't go out with him?"

"No, no, no. I'm just saying wear an old dress!"

Three old men were sitting around talking about who had the worst health problems. The 70 year old said, "Have I got a problem... Every morning I get up at 7:30 and have to take a major piss, but I have to stand in front of the toilet for an hour because my pee barely trickles out."

"Heck, that's nothing," said the eighty year old. "Every morning at 8:30 I have to take a huge dump, but I have to sit on the can for hours because of my chronic constipation. It's terrible."

The ninety-year-old said, "Oh, that's nothing! Every morning at 7:30 I piss like a racehorse and then at 8:30 I shit like a pig." The other two ask, "Well, what's the problem with that? He replied, "I don't wake up till eleven!"

An elderly man owned a farm in Louisiana with a large pond in the back. It was properly shaped for swimming, so he fixed it up with picnic tables and peach trees. One evening he walked down to his pond with a five-gallon bucket to bring back some fruit. As he neared the pond, he heard voices shouting and laughing with glee. Moving closer, he saw it was a bunch of young women skinny-dipping in his pond. Startled by his presence they quickly swam to middle of the pond. One of the women shouted to him, "We're not coming out until you leave!"

The old man frowned, "I assure you young ladies that I didn't come down here to watch you swim naked." Holding the bucket up he said, "I'm just here to feed the alligator."

The moral of the story is that some old men can still think quickly on their feet!!!

An old man and his wife were in bed. The old man farts and says, "Seven Points." His wife rolls over and says, "What the heck was that?" The old man replied, "Fart football... I just scored." A few minutes later the wife lets one go and says, "Touchdown, tie score."

A few minutes later the old man rips another fart and brags, "Touchdown, I'm ahead again; 14 to 7."

Not to be out done the wife rips another one and says, "Touchdown, tie score." Then, five seconds later she lets out a little squeaker and says, "Field goal, I lead 17 to 14!"

Now the pressure's on and the old man refuses to get beat by a woman so he strains real hard but to no avail. Realizing a defeat is unacceptable, he gives it everything he has, but instead of farting, he poops the bed. The wife looks and says, "What in the world was that?"

The old man replied, "Half-time, Switch sides!"

5

Religion

There are roughly 3500 different organized religions in the world - Christianity, Judaism, Buddhism, Hinduism, and Islam being among the largest. Though the specific tenets vary, the one thing they all have in common is that they're "faith based" with some sort of spiritual deity at the center of their ideologies. Even with all of our modern day technology and historical developments, scientists and theologians still cannot determine which religion, if any, are even remotely correct. The only hypothesis I think everyone can agree on is that we can pretty much rule out Scientology. Those guys are fucking nuts! Can I get an "Amen, brother?"

This is a tough chapter to include because so many people take religion so literally that even joking about it is deemed sacrilegious. If you are one of those people, you might want to skip this chapter and go read some more dick jokes. That said…

Jesus Christ walks into a hotel, puts a handful of nail down on the counter and asks the clerk, "Hey, could you put me up for the night?"

A priest is teaching a young altar boy to swim one day and the boy says, "Father, will I really sink if you take your finger out?"

Twelve priests were about to be ordained. The final test was for them to line up in a row totally nude, while a sexy, beautiful, big breasted, nude model danced before them. Each priest had a small bell attached to his "little Bishop" and they were told that anyone whose bell rang when she danced in front of them would not be ordained because he had not reached a state of spiritual purity.

The beautiful model danced before the first candidate, with no reaction. She proceeded down the line with the same response from all the priests until she got to the final priest, Carlos.

Poor Father Carlos... As she danced, his bell began to ring so loudly that it flew off clattering across the floor. Embarrassed, Carlos quickly scrambled to where the bell came to rest and bent over to pick it up. At that moment, all the other bells began to ring!

A priest was very fond of his flock of hens and a cockerel. He kept them in a coop behind the parish, but one Saturday night, the cockerel was missing. Suspecting "fowl" play, he decided to say something about it at church the next morning. During mass he asked the congregation, "Has anyone got a cock?"

Then all the men stood up. "No, no," he said, flustered, "That's not what I meant. Has anybody seen a cock?" All the women stood up.

"No, that's not what I meant either. Has anyone seen a cock that doesn't belong to them?" Half the women stood up.

Now, thoroughly embarrassed, he said, "Perhaps I should rephrase the question: has anybody here seen MY cock?" All the altar boys stood up.

A minister checks into a hotel room. He says to the front desk clerk, "I certainly hope the porn channel is disabled." The clerk frowns and says, "It's regular porn, you sick bastard!"

Two Muslim fundamentalists are sitting in a Gaza Strip bar chatting over a pint of goat's milk. One pulls his wallet out and flips to a picture. "This is my oldest son, Mohammed. He is a martyr." He flips to another photo, "And this is my youngest son, Ahmad – he is also a martyr."

The second fundamentalist sighs, "They blow up so fast, don't they?"

A guy is running late for the most important job interview of his life. He is circling the block, desperately trying to find parking spot but having no luck. He's not the least bit religious but this situation calls for some spiritual assistance. He looks to the sky, "Dear Lord, I know I have neglected you for many years but I am desperate and ready to be your humble servant. Please help me find a parking so I can make my interview on time. If you grant me this favor I vow to quit drinking, gambling, womanizing, and I'll even promise to go back to church every Sunday!"

And just like that, "poof" - a spot opens up. The guy immediately looks up to the heavens, "Never mind... I just found one."

A hooker approaches a priest walking down the street, "Hey Father, how 'bout a blow job?" Confused & shocked, the priest quickly bolts back to the parish. Later, when no one is around, he stops one of the nuns. "Excuse me Sister but what's a blowjob?"

She smiles, "Why Father, its fifty dollars. Same as it is downtown."

A 14 year old altar boy walks into a confessional; "Bless me Father, for I have committed a sin of the flesh with a very loose girl." The priest asks, "Is that you, little Johnny Parisi?" "Yes, Father, it is I" he replied. "And who was the girl you were with?" "I can't tell you, Father, I don't want to ruin her reputation." said Johnny. "Well, Johnny, I'm sure to find out her name sooner or later, so you may as well tell me now. Was it Tina Minetti?" -- "I cannot say."

"Was it Teresa Volpe?" – "I'll never tell."

"Was it Nina Capelli?" – "I'm sorry, but I cannot name her."

"Was it Cathy Piriano?" – "My lips are sealed."

"Was it Rosa D'Angelo, then?" – "Please, Father, I cannot tell you."

The priest sighs in frustration. "You're very loyal Johnny and I admire that. But you've sinned and must atone. You cannot be an altar boy now for 4 months. Now you go and pray."

Johnny walks back to his pew, and his friend Nino slides over and whispers, "So, what'd you get?"

He replied, "4 months vacation and five good leads!"

An Amish boy and his father were in a mall. They were amazed by everything they saw, but especially by two shiny, silver walls that could move apart and then slide back together again (an elevator to you & me). The boy asked, "What is this

Father?" He responded, "Son, I've never seen anything like this in my life."

While they watched in amazement, a fat old lady in a wheel chair rolled up to the moving walls and pressed a button. The walls opened and the lady rolled between them into a small room. The walls closed and the boy and his father watched the small circular numbers above the walls light up sequentially. They continued to watch until it reached the last number and then the numbers began to light in the reverse order. Finally the walls opened up again and a gorgeous 24-year-old blonde stepped out. The father said quietly to his boy, "Son, hurry up and go get your mother!"

A woman was having an affair during the day while her husband was at work. Her 9-year- old son came home unexpectedly, sees them and hides in the bedroom closet to watch. The woman's husband also came home. She puts her lover in the closet, not realizing that the little boy was in there already. The little boy says, "Dark in here." The man, startled, says, "Yes, it is." The boy says, "I have a baseball."

Man – "That's nice."   Boy – "Want to buy it?"

Man – "No, thanks."   Boy – "My dad's outside."

Man – "Okay, how much?"   Boy – "$250"

The next week, it happens again and the boy and the lover are in the closet together.

Boy - "Dark in here."   Man – "Yes, it is."

Boy – "I have a baseball glove."   Man - "How much?"

Boy – "$750"   Man – "Fine."

A few days later, the father says to the boy, "Grab your glove, let's go outside and have a game of catch." The boy says, "I can't, I sold my baseball and my glove." The father asks, "How much did you sell them for?" The boy said, "$1,000."

The father says, "That's terrible to charge your friends like that...that is way more than those things cost. I'm taking you to church and make you confess."

They go to the church and the father makes the little boy sit in the confession booth and he closes the door. The boy says, "Dark in here." The priest says, "Don't start that shit again!"

Minutes before confession is about to begin, Father Thomas rushes from the confessional and approaches one of his alter boys, "Matthew, my son, I have run out of holy water and must go get some more. I'd like you to start confessional for me. All you have to do is sit in the booth, the people will confess their sins, and you look them up in the book to decide their penance."

So Matthew sits in the booth and the first person comes in. "Forgive me Father for I have sinned," he says, "I stole a six pack of beer." Matt frantically looks through the book, "Hmm, stealing… ah here we are. Okay my son, do 10 rosaries and 5 Hail Mary's."

The next man comes into the booth. "Father, forgive me for I have sinned. I cheated on my wife again." Matt looks through the book "Adultery, adultery… here we go. All right my son, do 30 rosaries and 30 Hail Mary's."

The next man enters, "Father, forgive me for I have sinned," then pauses, choked up. "What is it my son, you can tell me anything." Finally, bursting into tears he laments, "I had anal sex."

Matt frantically looks through the book, "Sodomy, sodomy, its got to be in here!" But he can't find it so he whispers to his alter boy friend, "Billy, what does Father Thomas usually give for sodomy?"

Billy looks around then whispers back, "He usually gives me a Coke and a Mars Bar."

A cab driver picks up a nun. As she hops in the back seat, he looks in the rear view mirror and says, "Sister, I feel guilty saying this but I've always fantasized about being with a nun."

"Are you Catholic?" she asks.

"Yes I am." He responds.

"Pull over for a minute my son."

He pulls the cab over, hops in the back with her and she gives him the best blowjob he's ever had in his life. When he's done he says, "Sister, I've gotta tell you, I'm not really Catholic." She smiles, "Well, I have a confession to make also. My name is Ralph and I'm on my way to a costume party."

One day while he was at the track betting on the ponies and nearly losing his shirt, Mitch noticed a priest step out onto the track and bless the forehead of one of the horses lining up for the 4th race. Lo and behold that horse - a very long shot - won the race. Mitch was very interested to see what the priest did the next race.

Sure enough, the priest stepped onto the track as the horses lined up and placed a blessing on one of the horse's forehead. So Mitch made a beeline for the window, and bet on the horse.

Again, though it was another long shot, that horse also won the race. Mitch collected his winnings and anxiously waited to see which horse the priest would bless for the 6th race. Again, Mitch bet on it and it won!

As the day went on, every horse the priest blessed always came in first. Mitch began to pull in some serious money, and by the last race, he knew his dreams were going to come true. He went to the ATM, withdrew his life savings, and waited for the priest to bless the next horse.

The priest stepped onto the track before the last race and blessed the forehead, eyes, ears, and hooves of one of the horses. Mitch bet every cent, and watched the horse come in dead last.

Dumbfounded, he made his way to the track yelled at the priest, "What happened, Father? All day long you blessed horses and they won. The last race, you blessed a horse and he lost. Now, thanks to you, I've lost all my savings!"

The priest nodded wisely and said, "That's the problem with you Protestants -- you can't tell the difference between a simple blessing and Last Rites!"

Two nuns, Sister Mary and Sister Helen, are touring Europe in their car. They get to Transylvania and are stopped at a traffic light. Suddenly, a diminutive vampire jumps onto the hood of the car and hisses through the windshield. Sister Mary cries, "Help! What shall I do?"

Sister Helen says, "Quick, turn on the windshield wipers; that will get rid of the abomination." Sister Mary switches them on, knocking the vampire about, but he clings on and hisses again at the nuns.

"What shall I do now?" she shouts.

"Hit him with the windshield washer fluid. I filled it up with Holy Water in the Vatican." The vampire steams as the water burns his skin, but he clings on and hisses again.

"Now what?" shouts Sister Mary.

"Show him your cross." says Sister Helen.

Sister Mary opens the window and shouts: "HEY, GET OFF MY CAR YOU FUCKING ASSHOLE!!"

When Nuns are admitted to Heaven they go through a special gate and must make one last confession before they become angels. Several are lined up waiting to be absolved of their sins before they are made holy. "And so," says St. Peter, "have you ever had any contact with a penis?"

"Well," says the first Nun, "I once touched the tip of one with the tip of my finger."

"OK" says St. Peter, "Dip your finger in the holy water and pass on into heaven."

The next Nun admits, "Well, I, you know, sort of massaged one a bit."

St. Peter says, "Okay, rinse your hand in the holy water and pass on into heaven."

Suddenly there is some jostling in the line and one of the nuns is trying to cut in front. "Well now, what's going on here?" says St. Peter.

"Well, your Excellency," says the Nun, "If I'm going to have to gargle that stuff, I want to do it before Sister Mary Thomas sticks her ass in it!"

The Tax Office sent an agent to audit the Synagogue's books. While checking the books he said to the Rabbi, "I notice you buy a lot of candles; what do you do with the candle drippings?" "Good question." noted the Rabbi. "We save them and send them back to the candle makers, and every now and then they send us a free box of candles."

"Oh" replied the auditor, somewhat disappointed that his unusual question had a practical answer. But he continued in his obnoxious way, "What about all these bread-wafer purchases? What do you do with the crumbs?"

"Ah, yes" replied the Rabbi, realizing the inspector was trying to trap him with an unanswerable question. "We collect them and send them back to the manufacturers, and every now and then they send us a free box of bread wafers."

"I see" replied the auditor, thinking hard about how he could fluster the know-it-all Rabbi.

"Well Rabbi what do you do with the leftover foreskins from the circumcisions you perform?"

"Here too, we do not waste." answered the Rabbi. "What we do is save all the foreskins and send them to the Tax Office and about once a year they send us a complete prick!"

In the beginning, Adam asked the Lord for a mate. And God said, "I can give you the perfect companion but it will cost you an arm & a leg." Adam thought for a moment and said, "Well what can I get for a rib?"

St. Peter

A Christian and a Muslim arrive at the pearly gates at the same time. St. Peter asks the Christian, "What brings you here my son?" He replies, "I am here for Jesus!" St. Peter exclaims, "That is good my son. Please come enter the Kingdom of God."

So the Christian heads through the pearly gates and St. Peter turns to the Muslim. "And what are you here for my son?" Thinking quickly, the nervous Muslim says, "Um, I too am here for Jesus."

St. Peter turns around and yells, "Hey Jesus, your cab is here!"

Three guys died and went to heaven. St. Peter told them there was only room for one more person so whoever died the most bizarre death would be allowed in while the other two would have to wait. So the first guy says... "I suspected my wife was cheating on me so I came home early one day to catch her in the act. The shades were drawn; candles burning, soft music playing but I couldn't them anywhere.

Finally, I spot the guy hanging off the balcony. I pounded him with a hammer until he let go and fell three stories down. I thought he was dead but, no, he rolls over and gives me the finger.

Now I'm so pissed I have the strength of ten men. I grab the refrigerator and toss it over the balcony on top of this jerk, killing him. Well, I still couldn't find my wife. I was so distraught that I put a gun to my head and shot myself. Pretty bizarre huh?" St. Peter nods.

The second guy stands up. "You think that's bizarre? I was riding my exercise bike when a draft came in and blew the curtains through the spokes, sending me flying over my balcony. By a miracle, I manage to grab a hold of the balcony of my downstairs neighbor. As I'm pulling myself up, this guy starts whacking me with a hammer so I let go. When I hit the ground I flipped him off, started getting up, then I get smacked in the head with a refrigerator and die instantly. Now that's bizarre!!! St. Peter nods.

The third guy very casually says, "Check this out; I'm naked, in a refrigerator...."

*(You need the accent for this one... ex: L = R)

Three Asian men died (that's not the funny part) and were greeted by St. Peter in heaven. He explained, "We're very overcrowded here so, I have to screen you. Whoever can tell me the true meaning of Easter gets in. If not, you'll have to wait. The first Asian guy says, "Easter is time when big fat man in red suit fly all over world in a red sleigh with Rudolf a Red-nose reindeer giving chocolate Easter egg to boy and girl in chimney." St. Peter snaps, "Are you retarded? That's not even close. Get out of here!"

The second Asian says, "I know Easter; it is time when Pilgrims go to Plymouth Rock and paint Indian face and carve chocolate Easter bunny with family to Thank-a-giving!" St. Peter snaps again, "If it's possible, you're dumber than your friend. Go to hell and don't come back until you can define the true meaning of Easter!"

So the third Asian guy says, "Excuse my friends, they don't know Easter but I do... Easter is time when Jesus Christ die for all man sin..." St. Peter smiles, "Good, go on." He continues, "And da people put him in a tomb with a big rock in front for three days. And at end of third day they take big rock away and Jesus Christ is dead no more. Then, they have him come outside of tomb and if he see his shadow..."

A busload of black guys died (that's not the funny part) and went to heaven. When they got to the Pearly Gates, a stunned St. Peter said, "Uh, I wasn't expecting you. Wait right here." So he went into God's office, "Excuse me Lord but there's roughly 30 black men waiting at the Pearly Gates; what should I do?" God snapped, "Don't be racist! Go let them in!"

Ten minutes later St. Peter came back into God's office, "Excuse me Lord but they're gone."

"The 30 black men?" asked God.

St. Peter answered, "No, the Pearly Gates."

A couple married 60 years were far from rich but scraped by because they watched their pennies. Though old, they were in very good health due to the wife's insistence on health food and exercise. One day their plane crashed, sending them off to Heaven. They reached the pearly gates and St. Peter escorted them inside. He took them to a beautiful mansion, furnished in gold and fine silks, with a fully stocked kitchen and a waterfall in the master bath and said, "Welcome to Heaven, this will be your home now." The old man asked St. Peter how much all this was going to cost. "Why, nothing," Peter replied, "Remember, this is your reward in Heaven."

The old man looked out the window and right there he saw a championship golf course, finer and more beautiful than any ever-built on Earth. "What are the greens fees?" grumbled the old man. "This is heaven," St. Peter replied. "You can play for free, every day."

They went to the clubhouse and saw a lavish buffet with every imaginable cuisine laid out with free flowing beverages and a champagne fountain. St. Peter told the man, "This is Heaven, it is all free for you to enjoy." The old man looked around and glanced nervously at his wife.

"Well, where are the low fat foods and the decaffeinated tea?"

"That's the best part," St. Peter replied. "You can eat and drink as much as you like of whatever you like, and you will never get sick or fat. This is Heaven!"

The old man pushed, "No watching my diet? No gym to work out at? No testing my blood sugar or pressure?"

"Never again. All you do here is enjoy yourself." replied St. Peter.

The old man glared at his wife and said, "You and your God damn bran muffins. We could have been here ten years ago!"

A lady dies and goes to heaven. She is chatting with St.

Peter at the Pearly Gates when all of a sudden she hears the most awful bloodcurdling screams. "Don't worry about that," says St. Peter, "it's only someone having the holes bored in their shoulders for the wings." The lady looks around very uncomfortable. Soon there's more bloodcurdling screams, worse than before.

"Oh my goodness! Now what's happening?" she asks. "Not to worry," says St. Peter, they are just having their head drilled to fit the halo."

"I can't do this," says the lady, "I'm off to hell."

"You don't want to go there," calls St. Peter, "You'll be raped and sodomized!"

"Yeah," says the lady, "but I've already got the holes for that!"

Holy Q & A

Q: How do you get a nun pregnant?
A: Dress her up as an altar boy.

Q: Why do Jewish people wear Yarmulke's?
A: 'Cuz those little propellers cost extra.

Q: What's the difference between a Jewish mother and a terrorist?
A: You can negotiate with a terrorist.

Q: What did the Jewish child molester say to lure his next target?
A: "Hey kid, wanna' buy some candy?"

Q: How do you make a Jewish American Princess scream twice?

A: Fuck her in the ass then wipe your dick on the drapes.

Q. What's the difference between a Catholic wife and a Jewish wife?

A. A Catholic wife has real orgasms and fake jewelry.

Q: What happens when a Jewish guy with a hard-on walks into a wall?

A: He breaks his nose.

6

Race

Okay, shh! Look over your shoulder. Anyone in ear shot? No? Good. Even so, I'm still going to whisper this chapter. Remember all that stuff I said at the beginning of the book about "offending people" and "don't kill the messenger?" Yeah well, throw that out the window because I left out hundreds of well-known street jokes simply but because I didn't want to have to continually apologize or explain myself to people. Call me a pussy if you want, but the fact remains that I just can't publish the raciest of the racist joke for one reason and one reason only: I'm white!

That's not to say that this chapter isn't funny or lacks edginess. I pushed the limit as far as I thought I could and I'm quite sure some of the overly PC-types will still be offended anyway. Why? 'Cuz they're fags!

Irish

Q: Where does an Irish family go on vacation?
A: To another bar!

Q: How can you tell the Irish guy in a hospital ward?
A: He's the one blowing the foam off his bedpan.

Q: What is the difference between an Irish Wedding and an Irish Funeral?
A: One less drunk!

Q: Why do Scottish men wear kilts?
A: 'Cuz sheep can hear zippers! -- (*Yeah, I know that one is Scottish not Irish…but it's FOR the Irish reader. It also works for hillbillies if you just substitute the set-up with, "Why do rednecks wear button down jeans?"*)

An Irishman arrived at J.F.K. Airport and wandered around the terminal with tears streaming down his cheeks. An airline employee asked him if he was already homesick.

"No," replied the Irishman "I've lost all me luggage!"

"How'd that happen?" asked the employee.

The Irishman lamented, "The cork fell out!"

Murphy calls to see his mate Paddy who has a broken leg. Paddy says, "Me feet are freezing mate, could you run upstairs and get me slippers?"

"No bother," he says, and he runs upstairs and sees Paddy's two, stunning 19 year old twin daughters lying on their beds. "Hello 'dere lasses, your father sent me up here to shag ya' both."

"Fook off you liar!" they yelled.

"I'll prove it," Murphy says.

So he shouts down the stairs, "Both of them, Paddy?"

"Of course both of them, what's the use of fookin' just one?"

An Irish drunk stumbles into a confessional booth. The priest hears him enter but, nothing else. After a few minutes the priest bangs on the wall, "Hello, hello..." The Irish guy shoots back, "Forget it buddy, there's no paper in this one either!"

An Englishman, a Scotsman, and an Irishman walk into a pub. They proceed to each buy a pint of Guinness. Just as they were about to enjoy their creamy beverage three flies landed in each of their pints, and were stuck in the thick head. The Englishman pushed his beer away from him in disgust.

The Scotsman poured his beer on the ground until the fly fell out then continued drinking. The Irishman picked up the fly, held it out over the beer by its wings and yelled, "SPIT IT OUT! SPIT IT OUT YOU BASTARD!!!"

Brenda O'Malley is home making dinner when Officer Tim Finnegan arrives at her door. "Brenda, there's somethin' I have to tell ya'. There was an accident down at the Guinness brewery..."

"Oh, fer the love of Jesus, Mary, and Bono!" cries Brenda. "Please don't let it be bad news!"

"Brenda. Your husband Shamus is dead. I'm so sorry!"

"Dear Lord above, how'd it happen?"

"It was terrible, Brenda. He fell into a vat of Guinness Stout and drowned."

"Oh my sweet Jesus Tim, please tell me he at least went quickly?"

"Well, sadly no Brenda. Truth be told, he got out three times to pee!"

At the World Women's Conference, a speaker from England stood up: "Last year we spoke about being more assertive with our husbands. After the convention I went home and told my husband that I'd no longer cook for him; he'd have to do it himself. After the first day I saw nothing. After the second day I saw nothing. But after the third day I saw that he had cooked a wonderful roast lamb." The crowd cheered.

A woman from America stood up: "After last year's conference I told my husband that I'd no longer be doing his laundry; he'd have to do it himself. After the first day I saw nothing. After the second day I saw nothing. But after the third day I saw that he had done not only his own laundry but mine as well." The crowd cheered.

A woman from Ireland stood up: "After last year's conference I also went home and told my husband that I would no longer do his shopping; he'd have to do it himself. After the first day I saw nothing. After the second day I saw nothing. But after the third day I could see a little bit out of my left eye."

Irishman John O'Reilly hoisted his beer and said, "Here's to spending the rest of me life between the legs of me wife!" That won him the top prize at Shenanigan's Pub for the best toast of the night!

He went home and told his wife, Mary, "I won the prize for the best toast of the night." She said, "Aye, did ya' now? And what was your toast?" He said, "Here's to spending the rest of me life, sitting in church beside me wife." "Oh, that is very nice indeed, John!" Mary said.

The next day, Mary ran into one of John's drinking buddies on the street. He chuckled leeringly and said, "John won the prize the other night at the pub with a toast about you, Mary."

She said, "ye, he told me, and I was a bit surprised meself. You know, he's only been there twice in the last four years. Once he fell asleep, and the other time I had to pull him by the ears to make him come!"

Paddy had been drinking at his local Dublin pub for many hours. Mick, the bartender says, "Sorry Paddy, I have to shut you off." He replies "Okay Mick, I'll be on my way then." Paddy spins around on his stool and falls flat on his face. "Shite!" he says as he pulls himself up using the stool and dusts himself off.

He tries taking a step towards the door and falls on his face again. "Shite, Shite!" He belly crawls to the door and shimmies up to the door. He sticks his head outside, takes a deep breath of fresh air, and slides out onto the pavement. Again, he falls flat on his face. "Bi' Jesus... I'm fockin' focked!" he says.

So he crawls down the sidewalk to his house just a few doors down, shimmies up to the door and goes inside. Using just his arms, he pulls his way up the stairs to his bedroom and manages to flop into his bed and passes out cold. The next morning his wife comes in with a cup of coffee and says, "Well, well...did we have a bit of the drink last night?" Paddy says, "Ay dear, I sure was right pissed. But how'd you know?"

"Mick called. You left your wheelchair at the pub."

Two Irishmen were sitting at a pub having beer and watching the brothel across the street. They saw a Baptist minister walk into the brothel and one of them said, "Aye, 'tis a shame to see a man of the cloth goin' bad."

Then they saw a rabbi enter the brothel and the other Irishman said, "Aye, 'tis a shame to see that the Jews are fallin' victim to temptation as well."

Next, they see a catholic priest enter the brothel, and one of the Irishmen said, "What a terrible pity...one of the girls must be dying."

An Irish priest is driving down to New York and gets stopped for speeding in Connecticut. The state trooper smells alcohol on the priest's breath and then sees an empty wine bottle on the floor of the car. He says, "Sir, have you been drinking?"

"Just water," says the priest. The trooper says, "Then why do I smell wine?" The priest looks at the bottle and says, "Good Lord! He's done it again!"

Italian

Q: What did the Italian with Alzheimer's say?
A: "Eh, fageddabou—wha?"

Q: What would you call it when an Italian has one arm shorter than the other?
A: A speech impediment

Q: Hear about the Italian prospector?
A: He came into town yelling, "Ay, ah fongol!" (*"Found gold"* – get it? *Did I really have to explain that? Jeez...*)

Little Vito was sitting in class one day. All of a sudden he yelled out, "Miss Jones, I gotta take a piss!" She replied, "No, no, Vito. Urinate. Use it in a sentence, and you may go."

Vito thinks for a bit and then says, "Okay...you're an eight, but if you had bigger tits; you'd be a ten!"

One day, during grammar lessons, the teacher asked who could use the word "beautiful" in the same sentence twice correctly. First she called on little Suzie, who responded with, "My father bought my mother a beautiful dress, and she looked beautiful in it."

"Very good, Suzie!" replied the teacher. She then called on little Michael.

"My mommy planned a beautiful banquet, and everyone thought it was beautiful."

She said, "Excellent, Michael!" Then she reluctantly called on Vito.

Vito said, "Last night at the dinner table, my sister told my father that she was pregnant, and he said, 'Beautiful, just fucking beautiful!'"

Little Vito was sitting on a park bench munching on one candy bar after another. After the sixth one, a man on the bench near him said, "Son, you know eating all that candy isn't good for you. It will give you acne, rot your teeth, and make you fat."

Vito replied, "My grandfather lived to be 107 years old."

The man asked, "Did your grandfather eat six candy bars at a time?"

"No, but he minded his own fucking business!"

A couple attending an art exhibition at the National Gallery was staring at a portrait that depicted three very black and totally naked men sitting on a park bench. Two of the figures had black penises, but the one in the middle had a pink penis. The curator of the gallery realized that they were having trouble interpreting the painting and offered his assessment. He went on for nearly an hour explaining how it depicted the sexual emasculation of African-Americans in a predominately white, patriarchal society.

"In fact," he pointed out, "some serious critics believe that the pink penis also reflects the cultural and sociological oppression experienced by gay men in contemporary society."

After the curator left, an Italian man approached the couple and said, "Would you like to know what the painting is really about?"

"Now why would you claim to be more of an expert than the curator of the gallery?" asked the couple.

"Because I'm the guy who painted it," he replied. "In fact, there are no African Americans depicted at all. It's just three Italian coal-miners. The guy in the middle went home for lunch."

An 18 year old Italian girl, embarrassed and scared, tells her Mom that she is pregnant. Her mother screams, "Who was the pig that did this to you? I want to know right now!"

So the girl picks up the phone and makes a call. An hour later, a Ferrari pulls up to their house. A distinguished gentleman impeccably dressed in an Armani suit steps out and enters the house.

In the living room with the girl and her parents, he explains, "Your daughter has informed me of the problem. I can't marry her because of my personal family situation but I'll take full responsibility and will pay all costs & provide for your daughter for the rest of her life. Additionally, if a girl is born, I will bestow a Ferrari, 2 retail stores, a beachfront villa, and a $2,000,000 bank account. If a boy is born, I will leave a couple of factories and as well as a $4,000,000 bank account. However, should there be a miscarriage, what do you suggest I do?"

At this point, the father, who had remained silent, places a hand firmly on the man's shoulder and whispers in his ear, "You fuck her again!"

A man was having an affair with an Italian woman and she became pregnant. Not wanting to ruin his marriage, he agreed to pay her a large sum of money if she'd return to Italy to have the child in secret. If she stayed, he would still provide child support until the kid turned 18.

She agreed to go to Italy, but asked how to contact him when the baby was born. To keep it discrete, he told her to simply send a postcard and write "Spaghetti" on the back. He would then arrange for the child support payments to begin.

Nine months later he came home to his confused wife. "Honey" she said, "you received a very strange postcard today." "Okay, well just give it to me and I'll explain later." he replied.

She handed him the postcard and watched as he read it, turned white, and fainted.

On the card was written: "Spaghetti, Spaghetti, Spaghetti, Spaghetti, Spaghetti... Three with meatballs, two without. Send extra sauce!"

Every Friday night the Italian community holds a dance in the church basement. Gennaro seizes this opportunity to wear his new Botticelli leather shoes for the first time. He asks Sophia to dance and as they dance he asks her, "Sophia, do you wear red panties tonight?"

Startled, Sophia replies, "Yes, Gennaro, I do wear red panties tonight, but how do you know?"

Gennaro answers, "I see the reflection in my new Botticelli shoes."

Next he asks Rosa to dance, and after a few minutes he asks, "Rosa, do you wear white panties tonight?" Rosa answers, "Yes, Gennaro, I do, but how do you know that?"

He replies, "Because my dear, I see the reflection in my new Botticelli shoes."'

The evening is almost over and Gennaro asks Carmela to dance. During the dance his face turns red, "Carmela, be stilla' my heart; I see you wear no panties tonight, is this true?"

Carmela smiles coyly and answers, "Yes Gennaro, I wear no panties tonight."

Gennaro gasps, "Thanka' God, I thought I had a crack in my new Botticelli shoes!"

An elderly Italian man who lived on the outskirts of Rome went to church for confession. "Bless Me, Father for I have sinned. During World War II, a beautiful Jewish woman from our neighborhood knocked urgently on my door and asked me to hide her from the Nazis. So I hid her in my attic."

The priest replied, "That was a wonderful thing you did, and you have no need to confess that."

"But there is more to tell, Father. She started to repay me with sexual favors. This happened several times a week, and sometimes twice on Sundays."

The priest said, "That was a long time ago and two people under those circumstances can easily succumb to the weakness of the flesh. However, if you are truly sorry for your actions, you are indeed forgiven."

"Thank you, Father. That's a great load off my mind. I do have one more question."

"And what is that?" asked the priest.

"Should I tell her the war is over?"

Guido was on trial for date rape. All the evidence weighed against him. Before the closing arguments the judge asked one last question; "Guido, did you have consent?"

Guido smiled, "Sure your Honor! I had cunt-scent on my fingers, cunt-scent on my chin, cunt-scent on my tongue..."

Two Italian men get on a bus and engage in an animated conversation. The lady behind them ignores them at first, but her attention is galvanized when she hears one of the men say, "Emma come first. Den I come. Den two asses come together. I come once-a more. Den two asses, dey come together again. Next, I come again anna pee twice. Den a finally, I come a one last time."

"You're a horrible, foul-mouthed man!" she exclaimed indignantly. "In this country, we don't speak of such vulgar things in public places!"

"Hey, coola' down lady." says the Italian man. "Who's a talkin' vulgar? I just tella my friend here how to spella' Mississippi!"

An old Italian man lived alone in the country. One spring he wanted to start his tomato garden but it was too difficult for him because ground was too hard. His only son, Vincenzo, used to help him but was now in prison. The old man wrote a letter to his son:

Dear Vincenzo,
  Sadly, I won't be able to plant my tomatoes this year. I am getting too old to be digging up my garden plot. If you were here, my troubles would be over. I miss you and wish you were here to help me as you always did.
                                                              Love, Papa

The next day he received a letter from his son:

Dear Papa,
I'd do anything for you Papa, except dig up that gar-
den. That's where I buried the bodies.

Love, Vinnie

Early the next morning, FBI and local police arrived and dug up the entire garden plot without finding any bodies. They apologized to the old man and left. The next day the old man received another letter from his son:

Dear Papa,
Go ahead and plant the tomatoes now. That's the best
I could do under the circumstances.

Love, Vinnie

Black

Confucius Say: Hanging out with black man is best way to meet white woman.

That guy is so black... when he gets out of the car, the oil light comes on!

Q: What are the 5 penis sizes?
A: 'Small, medium, large, ouch," and, "Hey, does that come in white?"

This black guy walks into a bar with a beautiful, multicolored parrot on his shoulder. The bartender says, "Wow, that's amazing! Where did you get it?"

The parrot says, "Africa. There's millions of 'em!"

A couple was watching a Discovery Channel special about an African bush tribe whose men all had penises 24 inches long. When a male reaches a certain age, a string is tied around his penis and on the other end is a weight. After a while, the weight stretches the penis to 24 inches.

Later that evening as the husband was getting out of the shower; his wife looked down at him and said, "How about we try the African string-and-weight procedure?" The husband agreed and they tied a string and weight to his penis.

A few days later, the wife asked her husband "How is our little tribal experiment coming along?"

"Well dear, I'd say it looks like we're just about half way there." he replied.

"Wow, you mean it's grown to 12 inches?"

"No, it's turned black."

One late, rainy night, a man from India, a Jew and a black guy broke down along the side of the road. They wandered up to a farmhouse for assistance. The farmer said, "Well, nothing is open now but you can spend the night here. Unfortunately, I only have room for 2 people so one of you will have to sleep in the barn. The man from India said, "I'll go sleep in the barn. My two friends can stay in the house." And with that, he went out to the barn.

Five minutes later he knocked on the door. "I'm truly sorry kind sir, but there's a cow in the barn and it's against my religion to sleep under the same roof as the sacred cow."

The Jewish guy says, "That's okay, I'll go sleep in the barn." And he heads out.

Five minutes later he knocked on the door. "Oy vey, there's a pig in the barn and pork is forbidden in my religion. I am terribly sorry but I just cannot sleep in the barn with the pig."

The black guy says, "Man, you mutha fuckers is a bunch of pussies. I'll go sleep my ass out in the barn."

And sure enough, five minutes later there's another knock on the door. Standing there was the cow and the pig...

Leroy is a 20 year-old 5th grader. His is homework assignment was to use each of these vocabulary words in a sentence. Let's see how Leroy did:

Dictate – My bitch say my dictate good.

Hotel – I gave my girlfriend crabs, and the hotel everybody.

Income – I just got in bed wid my ho and income my wife.

Omelet – I should pop a cap in yo' ass, but omelet dis one slide.

Rectum – I had two Cadillac's, but my bitch rectum both.

Penis – I went to the doctor, he handed me a cup and said, "penis."

Foreclose – If I pay alimony today, I got no more money foreclose.

Undermine – There's a fine lookin' ho living in the apartment undermine.

Catacomb – I saw Don King the other night. Man, somebody get that catacomb.

Stain – My mother-in-law stopped by and I axed her, "Do you plan on stain for dinner?"

Acoustic – When I was little, my uncle bought me acoustic and took me to the pool hall.

Iraq – When we got to the pool hall, I told my uncle Iraq, you break.

Israel – Man, that Rolex is fake. Tito says, "Bullshit dawg that watch Israel!"

Disappointment – My PO said if I miss disappointment they gonna' send me back to the joint.

Yo Mamma

I've actually had someone give me shit before saying, "Why do you just assume 'yo mamma' jokes are for black people? That's racist!" Actually, they were originated by black people, about black people, for black people. But just in case some of you still disagree with me just pretend that these jokes are in the Irish section. Is that better, ya' wuss!

Yo Mamma is so fat...

Yo Mamma's so fat when she walked in front of the TV I missed 3 commercials

Yo Mamma's so fat the last time she saw 90210 was on the scale

Yo Mamma's so fat when she sat on a rainbow, Skittle's fell out.

Yo Mamma's so fat I had to take a train and two busses just to get on her good side.

Yo Mamma's so fat when she hauls ass, she has to make two trips.

Yo Mamma's so fat she's 36-24-36... but that's her forearm, neck, and thigh!

Yo Mamma's so fat she can lay down and stand up and her height doesn't change.

Yo Mamma's so fat the horse on her Polo shirt is real.

Yo Mamma's so fat when she ran away they had to use all four sides of the milk carton.

Yo Mamma's so fat she was born with a silver shovel in her mouth.

Yo Mamma's so fat her picture fell off the wall!

Yo Mamma's so fat her cereal bowl came with a lifeguard.

Yo Mamma's so fat I took her to a dance and the band skipped.

Yo Mamma's so fat every time she walks in high heels she strikes oil!

Yo Mamma's so fat she got tired climbing the escalator

Yo Mamma's so fat her blood type is Ragu!

Yo Mamma's so fat her high school picture was an aerial photograph.

Yo Mamma's so fat she qualifies for group insurance.

Yo Mamma's so fat she can smell bacon frying in Canada!

Yo Mamma's so fat she can use Mt. Everest for a dildo.

Yo Mamma's so fat she eats Wheat Thicks.

Yo Mamma's so fat she had to get out of bed to roll over.

Yo Mamma's so fat she has to lie down to tie her shoe.

Yo Mamma's so fat she put on her lipstick with a paint-roller!

Yo Mamma's so fat she rocked herself to sleep trying to get up.

Yo Mamma's so fat she rolled over 4 quarters and it made a dollar!

Yo Mamma's so fat she thinks a balanced meal is a ham in each hand.

Yo Mamma's so fat she thought gravy was a beverage.

Yo Mamma's so fat she went to the beach and sold shade!

Yo Mamma's so fat she went to the movies and sat next to everyone!

Yo Mamma's so fat she's got more chins than a Chinese phone book!

Yo Mamma's so fat she's on both sides of the family!

Yo Mamma's so fat when she turns around they throw her a welcome-back party.

Yo Mamma's so fat your family portrait has stretch marks.

Yo Mamma's so fat all restaurants in town have signs that say: "Maximum Occupancy: 240 Patrons or "Yo Momma!""

Yo Mamma is so ugly...

Yo Mamma's so ugly when she joined an ugly contest they said, "Sorry, no professionals."

Yo Mamma's so ugly she looked out the window and got arrested for mooning.

RACE

Yo Mamma's so ugly they filmed Gorillas in the Mist in her shower

Yo Mamma's so ugly when she walks into a bank they turn off the surveillance cameras

Yo Mamma's so ugly her momma had to be drunk just to breast feed her

Yo Mamma's so ugly she made an onion cry.

Yo Mamma's so ugly when she went to the beautician it took 12 hours... for a quote!

Yo Mamma's so ugly when she tried to take a bath, the water jumped out!

Yo Mamma's so ugly on Halloween the kids trick or treat her by phone!

Yo Mamma's so ugly her dentist treats her by mail!

Yo Mamma's so ugly it looks like she sleeps on a bed of nails face down!

Yo Mamma's so ugly she could curdle urine.

Yo Mamma's so ugly she could make a freight train take a gravel road.

Yo Mamma's so ugly she has to get her vibrator drunk first.

BATHROOM BITS

Yo Mamma's so ugly she has to sneak up on a cup of water!

Yo Mamma's so ugly that when she looks at a glass of milk it turns to cheese.

Yo Mamma's so ugly the psychiatrist makes her lie face down.

Yo Mamma's so ugly the tide won't even take her out.

Yo Mamma's so ugly they used her in prisons to cure sex offenders!!

Yo Mamma's so ugly when a baby, she was breast fed through a straw!

Yo Mamma's so ugly when a child, she had to be fed with a slingshot!

Yo Mamma's so ugly when she walks by the bathroom the toilet flushes.

Yo Mamma's so ugly when she was born her incubator windows were tinted.

Yo Mamma is so stupid...

Yo Mamma's so stupid she tried to drop acid but the car battery fell on her foot.

Yo Mamma's so stupid she thinks Taco Bell is a Mexican Phone Company.

Yo Mamma's so stupid she bought a pair of flip-flops and the bitch only got one toe!

Yo Mamma's so stupid she sold her car for gas money!

Yo Mamma's so stupid she ordered her sushi well done.

Yo Mamma's so stupid she tried to drown a fish.

Yo Mamma's so stupid on a job application, under "education" she put "Hooked on Phonics."

Yo Mamma's so stupid she got hit by a parked car.

Yo Mamma's so stupid she thought Sherlock Holmes was a housing project.

Yo Mamma's so stupid she thought asphalt was a skin disease.

Yo Mamma's so stupid when she saw the "NC-17" sign she went home and got 16 friends.

Yo Mamma's so stupid when she heard 90% of all accidents occur around the home, she moved.

Yo Mamma's so stupid she got fired from a blowjob.

Yo Mamma's so stupid I saw her standing on an empty bus.

Yo Mamma's so stupid it takes her 2 hours to watch 60 Minutes.

Yo Mamma's so stupid -it takes her a day to cook a 3-minute egg.

Yo Mamma's so stupid she jumped out the window and went up.

Yo Mamma's so stupid she saw a sign that said Wet Floor so she did!

Yo Mamma's so stupid she thought innuendo was an Italian suppository.

Yo Mamma's so stupid she thought manual labor was a Mexican!

Yo Mamma's so stupid she tried to hang herself with a cordless phone.

Yo Mamma's so stupid that when I asked her for a color TV she asked me what color.

Yo Mamma's so stupid she mailed me a fax with a stamp on it.

Yo Mamma's so stupid she took a ruler to bed to see how long she slept.

Yo Mamma's so stupid she asked for a price check at the Dollar Store.

Yo Mamma's so stupid she invented the "solar power flashlight."

Yo Mamma's so stupid when she heard 90% of all crimes occur around the home she moved.

Yo Mamma's so stupid when she missed the #44 Bus she took the #22 bus twice.

Latino

Q: Why did the Mexican school cancel driver's ed & sex ed in the same day?
A: The donkey died.

Q: How come they only sent 600 Mexicans to the Alamo?
A: They only had one car.

Q: What did Davy Crocket say when he saw all the Mexicans running towards the Alamo?
A: Who ordered concrete?

Q: Why should you never run over a Mexican riding a bike?
A: It's probably your bike!

Q: What do you call a Mexican with a new car?
A: A felon.

Q: What do you get when you cross a Puerto Rican and a black person?
A: Somebody too lazy to steal.

Q: What do you call two Mexicans playing basketball?
A: Juan-on-Juan.

Q: Why aren't there any Puerto Ricans on The Jetsons?
A: They don't work in the future either!

Q: What do you call a Mexican without a lawn mower?
A: Unemployed.

Q: What do you call a Mexican on a riding lawnmower?
A: Promoted.

Q: Why don't Mexicans play hide & seek?
A: No one will look for them.

Q: What is the difference between a Mexican and an elevator?
A: One can raise a child.

Q: Juan, Carlos, and Jose all jump off a cliff to see who will hit the ground first. Who wins?
A: Society.

Q: Did you hear about the winner of the Mexican beauty contest?
A: Me neither.

Q: What do you get when you cross a Mexican with an octopus?
A: I don't know but it could pick lettuce real good.

Q: Why don't Mexicans barbeque?
A: The beans fall through the little holes on the grill.

Q: What are the first 3 words in every Mexican cookbook?
A: Steal a chicken...

Q: What do you call a Mexican baptism?
A: Bean dip.

Q: Did you hear about the two car pile-up in the Wal-Mart parking lot?
A: 50 Mexicans died.

Q: What do you call 4 Mexicans in quicksand?
A: Quatro Cinco.

Q: Why do Mexican kids walk around school like they own the place?
A: Any Mexican that can run jump or swim is in the US!

Q: When you apply for Welfare in Mexico what does that Government give you?
A: A map of the United States

Pedro came to the US (illegally, of course) from Mexico. He was only there a few months when he became very ill. He went to doctor after doctor, but none could help him. Finally, he went to an Afghani doctor who said, "Take dees bocket, go into de odder room, crap in de bocket, piss on de crap, and den put your head down over de bocket and breathe in de fumes for ten minutes."

So Pedro took the bucket, went into the other room, crapped in the bucket, pissed on the shit, bent over and breathed in the fumes for ten minutes. Coming back to the doctor he said, "It worked, Amigo. I feel so good! What was wrong with me?"

The doctor said, "You were homesick."

Jose and Carlos are panhandlers in different parts of town.

Carlos panhandles just as long as Jose but only collects $2 to $3 every day. Jose brings home a suitcase FULL of $10 bills, drives a Mercedes, lives in a mortgage free house and has lots of money to spend. Carlos asks Jose, "I work just as long and hard as you do but how do you bring that much money every day?"

Jose says, "Look at your sign, what does it say?" Carlos sign reads, "I have no work, a wife and six kids to support." Jose says, "No wonder you only get $2-3 dollars." Carlos asks, "Well, what does your sign say?"

Jose shows Carlos his sign – "I only need another $ 10 to move back to Mexico!"

Polish

Q: How do you set up a Polish guy in a nice small business?
A: You put him in a big business and wait...

Q: What do polish lesbians use as lubricant?
A: Tarter sauce.

Q: Did you hear about the Polish hockey team?
A: They drowned during spring training.

A Polish family is sitting around the house one afternoon. The wife says to her husband, "Let's send the kids outside to 'P – L – A – Y' so we can go into the bedroom and fuck!"

An Italian guy and a Polish guy get jobs working for the phone company putting in telephone poles. After the first day the foreman asks, "How many poles did you put in?" The Italian guy says, "Twelve" and the Polish guy says, "Two." "Two!?" cried the foreman, "the Italian put in twelve!"

The polish guy replies, "Yeah, but you should see how far his are sticking out of the ground!"

A Polish woman is swerving down the road when a cop pulls her over and says, "License and registration!" He checks out her license for a minute then asks, "Polish huh?" She sighs, "Yes."

So the cop smiles and starts undoing his zipper. She shrieks, "Oh no, not another damn breath-a-lizer!"

An Irishman, an Italian, and a Polish guy all apply for the same job. The interviewer has no ears. The Irishman goes in first. The interviewer says, "Sir, this job requires the powers of observation. Make an observation about me." The Irish guy says, "Well, ya' got no ears."

"Get out!" the interviewer screamed. The Italian goes in next. The guy says, "This job requires the powers of observation so, make one about me."

The Italian says, "Eh, I 'a see that you gotta no ears." "Get the hell out!" screamed the interviewer.

The Italian goes up to the Polish guy waiting for the interview, "Hey man, da' boss in there gotta no ears and he's a little bit 'a sensitive about it. So whatever you 'a do, don't mention it!"

The Polish guy says, "Don't worry."

The interviewer says to the Polish guy, "This job requires the powers of observation. Make an observation about me."

The Polish guy thinks for a minute then says, "Well, you wear contact lenses."

"That's right. Great observation!" said the boss. "How did you notice that?"

The Polish guy says, "Well, how can you wear glasses? You got no fuckin' ears!"

One day this Polish guy stranded on a desert island for ten years sees an unusual speck on the horizon. As the speck gets closer, he begins ruling out the possibility of it being a ship, small boat, or even a raft. Suddenly, emerging from the water was a drop-dead gorgeous blonde, wearing a wet suit and scuba gear.

She approaches him; "How long has it been since you've had a cigarette?"

"Ten years!" the stunned man says. She unzips a waterproof pocket on her sleeve and pulls out a pack of Camels. He lights one up and takes a long drag, savoring the smoke. "Man, is that good!"

She then asks, "How long has it been since you've had a taste of Bourbon?"

Trembling, he replies, "Ten years!" She reaches into another pocket, retrieves a flask of Bourbon, and hands it to him.

He takes an enormous gulp. "Wow, this is amazing!" Then she starts slowly, seductively, taking off her wet suit. "How long has it been since you played around?"

With tears in his eyes, he says, "Sweet Lord above! Don't tell me you've got golf clubs in there!"

An Irishman, a Mexican and a Polish guy were working on scaffolding on the 20th floor of a building. As they were eating lunch the Irishman said, "Corned beef and cabbage! Christ, if I get this crap for lunch one more time I swear I'm going to jump off this building."

The Mexican opened his lunch box and exclaimed, "Burritos again! If I get burritos one more time; I'm also going to jump off!"

The Polish guy opened his lunch, "Bologna again? If I get bologna one more time I'll jump too."

The next day the Irishman opened his lunch, saw corned beef and cabbage and jumped to his death. The Mexican opened his lunch, saw a burrito and jumped too. The Pollack opened his lunch, saw the bologna and jumped to his death as well.

At the funeral the Irishman's wife was weeping. She said, "If I'd known how sick of corned beef and cabbage he was I never would've given it to him!" The Mexican's wife said, "I didn't realize he hated burritos so much. I should have given him tacos or enchiladas!"

Everyone turned and stared at the Polish guy's wife. She shrugged her shoulders, "Hey, don't look at me. He makes his own lunch!"

Redneck

I know "redneck" isn't technically a race – it's more of a "lifestyle choice" but I felt this was the perfect chapter to slide these in. Comedian Jeff Foxworthy and his Blue Collar compatriots pretty much have cornered the market when it comes to redneck/hillbilly street jokes. In fact, as of this printing, there are only a select few of these street jokes left out there that Larry the Cable Guy hasn't slid into his act and tried to pass off as his own. I'd like to get them out there before he does!

Hillbilly Q&A

Q: How can you tell if a redneck is married?
A: There's dried tobacco juice on both sides of his pickup truck.

Q: Why did they raise the minimum drinking age in Arkansas to 32?
A: They want to keep alcohol out of the high schools.

Q: What do they call reruns of Hee Haw in Alabama?
A: Documentaries.

Q: What happens when a hillbilly couple gets divorced?
A: By law, they are still cousins.

Q: How do you know when you're staying in a Hillbilly hotel?
A: When you call the front desk to say, "I gotta' leak in my sink," the clerk replies, "Go ahead!"

Q: Why was the toothbrush invented in West Virginia?
A: If it were anywhere else, it'd have to be called a teeth brush!

Q: How do you circumcise a guy from Kentucky?
A: Kick his sister in the teeth.

A Mississippi State trooper pulls over a pickup on I-75 and asks the driver, "Got any ID?" The driver replies, "'Bout what?"

A police officer came upon a hillbilly who was making wild love to a cow. Startled and stunned, the police officer screamed, "What in the hell are you thinking about, man!!??"
The hillbilly coyly replied, "Uh, a younger and hotter cow!

When a guy walks into a Louisiana bar and orders a mudslide, all the patrons glare at him. The bartender curiously asks,

"You ain't from 'round here, is ya'?" He replies, "Nope, I'm from Pennsylvania."

"Well now, so just what is it do ya' do up yonder in that thar' Pennsylvania?"

"I'm a taxidermist."

The bartender, now very bewildered asks, "What in tarnation is a tax-e-derm-ist?" The man explains, "I mount animals."

The bartender stands back and hollers to the whole bar, "It's okay boys, he's one of us!"

A farmer walks into his bedroom with a sheep under his arm and says, "Darling, this is the pig I have sex with when you have a headache."

She looks up from her pillow and says, "I think you'll find that's a sheep, you idiot."

He says, "I think you'll find I wasn't talking to you."

A lady went into a bar in Waco and saw a cowboy with his feet propped up on a table. He had the biggest boots she'd ever seen. She asked if it was true what they say about men with big feet being well endowed. The cowboy grinned, "Shore is, little lady. Why don't you come on out to the bunkhouse and let me prove it to you?"

Wanting to find out for herself, she spent the night with him. The next morning she handed him a $100 bill. Blushing, he said, "Well, thankee, ma'am. Ah'm real flattered. Ain't nobody ever paid me fer my services before."

"Don't be flattered... take the money and buy yourself some boots that fit!!!"

A small zoo in Alabama obtained a very rare species of

female gorilla. Within a few weeks the gorilla became very difficult to handle and the vet determined the problem; the gorilla was in heat. To make matters worse, there was no male gorilla available. Dwelling on their problem, the Zoo Keeper thought of Billy-Bob Walton; the guy who for cleaned the animal cages.

Billy-Bob, like most rednecks, had little sense but possessed the ability to satisfy a female of any species. The Zoo Keeper approached him with a proposition. "Would you be willing to mate with our gorilla for $500.00?" He hemmed and hawed at first and finally said he'd have to think it over.

The next day he announced he'd accept their offer only under the following four conditions:

"First, I ain't gonna' kiss her on the lips." The Zoo Keeper quickly agreed.

"Second, you can't never tell no one about this." He agreed again.

"Third, I want all the childrin' raised Southern Baptist." Once again it was agreed.

Finally, Billy-Bob stated, "You gotta' give me another week to come up with the $500!"

An Idaho farmer drove his pickup to a neighboring farm and knocked at the door. After a few minutes a young boy answered and the farmer asked, "Is your Pa home?"

"No sir, he ain't," the boy replied. "He went into town."

"Welp, is your Ma here?"

"No sir, she ain't here neither. She went into town with Pa."

"How about yer brother, Howard? Is he here?" "Nope. He went with Ma and Pa."

The farmer stood there for a few minutes, shifting from one foot to the other mumbling to himself.

"Is there anything else I can do fer ya?" the boy asked politely.

"Welp," said the farmer uncomfortably, "I really need to talk to yer Pa about your brother Howard getting my daughter, Pearly Mae pregnant." The boy considered for a moment.

"You would have to talk to Pa about that. If'n it helps you any, I know Pa charges $50 for the bull and $25 for the hog, but I really ain't know how much he gets fer Howard."

A southern gas station owner was trying to increase sales so he put up a sign; "Free Sex with Fill-Up!" Soon a local redneck pulled in, filled his tank and asked for his free sex. The owner told him to pick a number from 1 to 10. If he guessed correctly he'd get his free sex.

The redneck guessed "eight" and the proprietor said, "Ooh, you were close. The number was seven. Sorry, no sex this time."

A week later, the same redneck, along with his pal Bubba, pulled in for another fill-up. Again he asked for his free sex. The proprietor again gave him the same story, and asked him to guess the correct number. The redneck guessed "two" this time. The proprietor said, "Sorry, it was three. Again you were close, but no free sex this time."

As they were leaving, the redneck said, "That game is rigged. He don't really give away free sex."

Bubba replied, "It ain't rigged, Billy Ray. My wife won twice last week!"

Redneck Pickup Lines…

Did you fart? 'Cuz you just blew me away!

Are your parents retarded? 'Cuz you sure are special.

My Love for you is like diarrhea - I just can't hold it in.

If you and I were Squirrels, I'd store my nuts in your hole.

Is there a mirror in your pants? 'Cuz I can see myself in 'em.

I may not be Fred Flintstone, but I bet I can make your bed-rock.

If you're going to regret this in the morning, we can sleep until the afternoon.

Your face reminds me of a wrench, every time I think of it my nuts tighten up.

Can you help me find my coon dog? I think he went into this cheap motel room.

You might not be the best looking girl here, but beauty is only a light switch away.

Random Race Jokes

A Chinese couple gave birth to a black baby. They named him 'Sum-Tin Wong'.

A Chinese couple is lying in bed and the husband turns to her and says, "I want 69!" She replies, "Why you want beef & broccoli now?"

Tonto, ear pressed to the ground, tells the Lone Ranger, "Buffalo come!" "How do you know?" asked the Lone Ranger. Tonto stands up and says, "Ear all sticky."

A girl says to her mother, "Mom, I want to marry this guy Nick. He's Greek." The mother says, "Okay dear, just don't ever let him flip you over! That's how Greek men are."

So she marries Nick and one night a few months later he asks, "You wanna' flip over?"

She quickly shoots back, "Absolutely not! My mother told me to never flip over for you!"

Nick says, "What's the matter? I thought you wanted to have kids?"

It was late one fall and the Indians on a remote South Dakota reservation asked their new chief if the coming winter was going to be cold or mild. Since he was a chief in a modern society, he had never been taught the old secrets. When he looked at the sky, he couldn't tell what the winter was going to be like. Nevertheless, to be on the safe side, he told his tribe that the winter was indeed going to be cold and that the members of the village should collect firewood to be prepared.

But being a practical leader, he got an idea. He went to a phone booth, called the National Weather Service and asked if the coming winter was going to be cold. "It looks like this winter is going to be quite cold" the meteorologist responded. So the chief went back to his people and told them to collect even more firewood in order to be prepared.

A week later, he called the National Weather Service again. "Does it still look like it is going to be a very cold winter?" "Yes," the meteorologist again replied, "it's going to be a very cold winter." The chief went back to his people and ordered them to collect every scrap of firewood they could find.

Two weeks later, the chief called the National Weather Service again. "Are you absolutely sure that the winter is going to be very cold?" "Absolutely," he replied. "It's looking more and more like it is going to be one of the coldest winters we've ever seen."

"How can you be so sure?" the chief asked.

The meteorologist said, "Because the Indians are collecting a shitload of firewood!"

Random Race Q&A

Q: What do you call a white guy surrounded by 20 Indians?
A: Bartender.

Q: Why did the Indian cross the road?
A: To sleep in the other ditch.

Q: What do you get when you cross Monica Lewinsky with a Native American?
A: A blown "injun."

Q: What do you call a German tampon?
A: A twatstika.

Q: A Black, a Mexican, and a Puerto Rican are in a car; who's driving?
A: The cop.

Q: What do you call 3 Asians driving a Camero?
A: The gooks of Hazard.

Q: Why did Disney World fail in Japan?
A: No one was tall enough to go on the rides!

Q: How do you swat 200 flies at one time?
A: Hit an Ethiopian in the face with a frying pan.

Q: What's so good about an Ethiopian blowjob?
A: You know she'll swallow.

Q: How many Ethiopians can you fit into a phone booth?
A: All of 'em.

Q: Why are aspirin white?
A: You want 'em to work, don't you?

Q: What happened when two Jews walked into a crowded bar?
A: They bought it.

A Somali arrives in Los Angeles as a new immigrant to the United States. He stops the first person he sees walking down the street and says, "Thank you Mr. American for letting me in this country!" But the passer-by says "You are mistaken, I am Mexican."

The man goes on and encounters another passer-by. "Thank you for having such a beautiful country here in America." The person says "I no American, I Vietnamese."

The new arrival walks further and the next person he sees he stops, shakes his hand and says, "Thank you for the wonderful America!" He puts up his hand and says "I am not an American, I'm Middle Eastern."

He finally sees a nice lady and asks suspiciously, "Are you

an American?" She says, "No, I am from Russia!" Puzzled, he asks her, "Where are all the Americans?"

The Russian lady looks at her watch, shrugs, and says, "I dunno, probably at work."

Believe it or not, Mujibar was actually trying to get into America legally. The Immigration Officer said, "Mujibar, you have passed all but one test. Unless you pass it you cannot enter America." Mujibar said, "I am happy now for the taking of your testing please sir."

The officer said, "Make a sentence using the words Green, Pink, and Yellow." After thinking for a few minutes and Mujibar said, "Okay, mister sir, I am to be ready."

The Officer said, "Go ahead." Mujibar confidently replied, "The telephone goes green, green, green, I pink it up, and say, yellow, this is Mujibar."

Mujibar now lives in a neighborhood near you and works as a Telephone Customer Support Rep for Bank of America.

7

Dumb Blondes

(as if there were any there kind…)

Some were the prom queen. Some were runners-up in the Miss Teen USA pageant. Some were the cheerleaders everyone in high school wanted to nail but never could have. These young women were not interested in high school boys. Eeew!

Instead, they sought the attention of older men; namely Mr. Ramsey, the substitute English Lit teacher (who actually did nail them). They grew up in ultra conservative, wealthy, and white suburbs. For their "sweet sixteen" they received a SAAB Turbo 900. Many are complete bitches with egos the size of Texas but rarely do they ever called out for that. Why? Because they're hot. Wicked hot!

Blondes Q&A

Q: Why are there so many blonde jokes?

A: So brunettes & redheads have something to do on the weekends.

Q: What's a blonde put behind her ears to attract men?
A: Her legs.

Q: What the first thing a blonde says in the morning?
A: Are you guys all on the same team?

Q: What did the blonde's mother says before she went on a date?
A: If you're not in bed by ten, come home!

Q: A blonde, a brunette, and a redhead are in third grade. Who has the biggest tits?
A: The blonde, because she's 18.

Q: What's the difference between a blonde and a washing machine?
A: A washing machine doesn't follow you around after you dump a load into it.

Q: Why did the blonde snort artificial sweetener?
A: She thought it was diet coke.

Q: What do you call a smart blonde?
A: A Golden Retriever.

Q: What did the blonde ask when her doctor told her she was pregnant?
A: "Is it mine?"

Q: Why do blondes get confused in the ladies room?
A: 'Cuz they're not used to pulling their own pants down.

Q: Why did the blonde tip-toe past the medicine cabinet?
A: So she wouldn't wake up the sleeping pills.

Q: What did the blonde's left leg say to her right leg?
A: Nothing. They have never met.

Typical Blonde's Year in Review

What a crazy year!!

<u>January</u> – Took new scarf back to store because it was too tight

<u>February</u> – Fired from pharmacy job for failing to print labels. Helloooo... bottles won't fit in typewriter!

<u>March</u> – Got really excited... finished jigsaw puzzle in 6 months... box said "2-4 years!"

<u>April</u> – Trapped on escalator for hours... power went out!!!

<u>May</u> – Tried making Kool-Aid, wrong instructions, 8 cups of water won't fit into those little packets!!!

<u>June</u> – Tried to go water skiing... couldn't find a lake with a slope.

<u>July</u> – Lost breast stroke swimming competition... learned later the other swimmers cheated; they used their arms!!!

<u>August</u> – Got locked out of my car in rain storm... car drenched because soft-top was open.

<u>September</u> – The capital of California is "C" isn't it???

<u>October</u> – Hate M &M's... they are so hard to peel!

<u>November</u> – Baked turkey for 4 1/2 days. Instructions said 1 hour per pound and I weigh 108!!!

<u>December</u> – Couldn't call 911... duh... there's no "eleven" button on the stupid phone!!!

A brunette says to her blonde friend, "My husband had really bad dandruff, so I gave him *Head & Shoulders*." The blonde says, "How do you give shoulders?"

A blonde pushes her BMW into a gas station and tells the mechanic it just died. After working on it for a few minutes, he got it idling smoothly. She says, "What was the problem?"

He replies, "Oh, nothing really; just shit in the carburetor."

She asks, "How often do I have to do that?"

A blind guy walks into a bar and tells the bartender that he has a great blonde joke. The bartender says, "Before you go any further, I have to tell you that I'm blonde, the two big guys sitting on each side of you are blonde, and the two bikers playing pool, they're blonde too. You still want to tell your joke?"

The blind guy says, "No, I guess you're right. I'd hate to have to explain it five times."

A blonde heard that milk baths would make her beautiful so she left a note for her milkman to leave 15 gallons of milk. When he read the note he figured there must be a mistake. He knocked and when she came to the door he said, "I found your note to leave 15 gallons of milk. Did you mean 1.5 gallons?"

She answered, "No, I want 15 gallons. I'm going to fill up my tub with it and have a milk bath."

The milkman asked, "Do you want it pasteurized?"

"No," she said, "just up to my tits."

Two blondes from Oklahoma were sitting on a park bench enjoying the beautiful day. One blonde says to the other, "Hey, what do you think is farther away; Florida or the moon?"

The other one says, "Hellooooooooooo, can you see Florida?????"

A blonde went into a worldwide message center to send a greeting to her mother overseas. When the man told her it would cost $300, she exclaimed, "But I don't have that much money. But I'd do anything to get a message to my mother."

Arching his eyebrow he asked, "Anything?" "Yes, yes, anything" she promised.

"Well, then, just follow me" he said as he walked towards the next room. "Come in and close the door." She did. He then said, "Now get on your knees and pull down my zipper." She did. "Now go ahead... take it out." She reached in and grabbed it with both hands, then paused.

The man closed his eyes and whispered, "Well ... go ahead."

She slowly opened her mouth, held it close to her lips, and then tentatively said, "Hello, Mom, can you hear me?"

A blonde gets on a plane and goes up to first-class. The flight attendant tells her that she'll have to move back because her ticket is not for first class. She says, "I'm blonde, I'm beautiful, and I'm going to California." The head flight attendant comes over and explains that she will have to move but again she says, "I'm blonde, I'm beautiful, and I'm going to California."

The attendant tells the pilot. He comes in and looks the situation over. He leans over and whispers something to the blond and she gets up immediately and moves out of first class. The attendants are flabbergasted, "What did you say to her?"

"I just told her that this section of the plane doesn't go to California!"

The blonde was terrified when she left work and walked out into a blinding snowstorm. Getting in her car, she remembered the advice her father gave her; "Wait for a snowplow to pass then, get right behind him. He'll pave the way and you'll be perfectly safe."

So she waited for a couple hours until a snowplow finally passed. Then she quickly pulled out and followed it around for a few more hours before the truck pulled over. The snowplow driver got out and approached her car. "Ma'am is there a problem?" he asked.

"No" she replied. "It's just that I wanted to get behind you so I wouldn't be so scared driving in this snow. Do you mind if I keep following you?"

He smiled, "Not at all! But I'm done with the K-Mart parking lot now. I've gotta go do the Wal-Mart one next..."

A guy walked into a bar with a pet alligator by his side. He put the alligator up on the bar and turned to the astonished patrons. "I'll make you a deal: I'll open this alligator's mouth and place my genitals inside. Then the gator will close his mouth for one minute. He'll then open his mouth and I'll remove my unit unscathed. In return for witnessing this spectacle, each of you will buy me a drink."

The crowd murmured their approval. The man stood up on the bar, dropped his trousers, and placed his privates in the alligator's mouth. The gator closed its mouth as the crowd gasped.

After a minute, the man grabbed a beer bottle and rapped the alligator hard on the top of its head. The gator opened his mouth and the man removed his genital, unscathed as promised.

The crowd cheered and the first of his free drinks was delivered. The man stood up and made another offer: "I'll pay anyone $100 who's willing to give it a try." A hush fell over the crowd.

After a while, a hand went up in the back of the bar and a blonde woman timidly spoke up, "I'll try, but you have to promise not to hit me on the head with the beer bottle."

Fresh out of college, a blonde began her new job as an elementary school counselor. One day at recess she noticed a boy standing by himself at the end of a field while all the other kids played soccer. Feeling sorry for him, she walked over and said, "Hi. I'm new here too. Would you like to be my friend?" He said, "Uh... sure."

She then asked, "So, why are you standing here all alone." He replied, "Because I'm the fucking goalie!"

A police officer stops a blonde for speeding and asks her very nicely if he could see her license. She replied in a huff, "I wish you guys would get your act together. Just yesterday you take away my license and then today you expect me to show it to you!"

A highway patrolman pulled alongside a speeding car on the freeway. Glancing at the car, he was astounded to see that the blonde behind the wheel was knitting! Realizing that she was oblivious to his flashing lights and siren, the trooper cranked down his window, turned on his bullhorn and yelled, "PULL OVER!"

"NO!" she yelled back, "IT'S A SCARF!"

A Russian, an American, and a blonde were talking one day. The Russian said, "We were the first people in space!" The American said, "We were the first people to land on the moon!" The Blonde said, "So what? We are going to be the first people to land on the sun!"

The Russian and the American looked at each other and shook their heads. "You can't land on the sun, dummy! You'll burn up!"

She replied, "We're not stupid, you know. We're going at night!"

A blonde was playing Trivial Pursuit one night. She landed on Science & Nature. Her question was, "If you are in a vacuum and someone calls your name, can you hear it?"

She thought for a minute then asked, "Is it on or off?"

A girl was visiting her blonde friend, who had acquired two new dogs, and asked her what their names were. The blonde responded by saying that one was named Rolex and the other was named Timex. Her friend said, "Whoever heard of someone naming dogs like that?"

She answered, "Helloooo… They're watch dogs!"

Two blondes got lost at the mall. They go to the map where a red arrow says: "YOU ARE HERE."

One looks at the other and exclaims, "Wow! How do they know that?"

A blonde woman named Cindy was having deep financial problems. So she got on her knees and prayed, "Dear God, please let me win the lottery. I really need your help or I'll loose my car, the house, and everything else." She doesn't win. The next day she prays again, "Dear God,

I really, really need your help! Please let me win the lottery or I'll loose my car, the house, and everything else." Once again, she doesn't win.

The next day, while praying again, God speaks to her, "Cindy, work with me here, BUY A DAMN TICKET!!"

A blonde went to a flight school and insisted she wanted to learn to fly that day. As all the planes were in use, the owner agreed to instruct her on how to pilot the helicopter solo by radio. He took her out, showed her how to start it and gave her the basics, and sent her on her way. After she climbed 1000 feet, she radioed in. "I love it! The view is so beautiful, and I'm starting to get the hang of this."

After 2000 feet, she radioed again, saying how easy it was becoming to fly.

The instructor watched her climb over 3000 feet, and was beginning to worry that she hadn't radioed in. A few minutes later, he watched in horror as the helicopter crashed about half a mile away.

He ran over to the wreckage and pulled her out. When he asked what happened, she said, "I don't know! Everything was going fine, but as I got higher, I started getting cold. I can't remember anything after I turned off the big fan."

A blonde suspects that her boyfriend is cheating on her, so she goes out and buys a gun. She goes to his apartment that same day and sure enough, when she opens the door, she finds her boyfriend in the arms of a redhead. She points the gun at her boyfriend at stares him down for a moment. Then, suddenly, she's overcome with grief, so she puts the gun up to the side her head.

Her boyfriend screams, "Honey, don't do it!!!"

The blonde yells back, "Shut up! You're next!"

A blonde goes into a library and cheerfully says, "Hi! I'm here to see the doctor!" In a stern but hushed voice, the librarian says, "Lower your voice Miss. This is a library!"

So the blonde whispers, "Oh sorry! I'm here to see the doctor."

This bar had a great new novelty item; a magic mirror that, if you told a lie, it would suck you in. One day a brunette walked up to the mirror and said, "I think I'm the most beautiful woman in the world" and the mirror immediately sucked her in.

The next day a redhead walked up to the mirror and said, "I think I'm the most beautiful woman in the world" and it promptly sucked her in.

Then the next day a blond walked up to the mirror and said, "I think--" and it sucked her in.

One day a blonde was walking along the lake shore and she spotted another blonde on the opposite shore. She cupped her hands together and shouted, "How do I get to the other side?"

The other blonde cupped her hands together and yelled back, "You are on the other side!"

Three women escaped from prison: a redhead, a brunette, and a blonde. They ran for miles until they came upon an old barn and decided to hide in the hayloft and rest. When they climbed up, they found three gunnysacks and decided to put them over their heads for camouflage.

An hour later the sheriff and his deputy came into the barn. The sheriff told his deputy to go up and check out the hayloft. When he got there the sheriff asked him what he saw.

He replied, "Just three gunnysacks." The sheriff told him to find out what was in them, so the deputy kicked the first bag, which had the redhead in it, and she said, "Bow-wow." So the deputy told the sheriff there was a dog in the first one.

Then he kicked the one with the brunette in it and she said, "Meow." The deputy told the sheriff there was a cat in the second one.

Then he kicked the one with the blonde in it and there was no sound at all, so he kicked it again. Finally, the blonde softly said, "Potatoes."

A British Airways employee got a call from a blonde, "How long is the Concorde flight from London to New York?" He politely said, "Um, just a minute, if you please." Then, as he turned to check the exact flight time, he heard an equally polite, "Thank you!" as the phone went dead.

Two blondes enter a department store, approach the perfume counter and pick up a sample bottle. Nancy sprays it on her wrist and smells it, "That's quite nice, don't you think, Kathy?" Kathy takes a sniff and replies, "Wow! You're right. That is really nice. What's it called?"

The sales clerks says, "It's called Viens a' moi – it means 'Come to Me' in French."

Nancy takes another sniff, then offers her arm to Kathy again and says, "Hmm, that doesn't smell like cum to me. Does it smell like cum to you?"

Okay, not all blondes are "special"

A guy in a supermarket notices a beautiful blonde wave at him and say hello. He's rather taken back, because he can't place where he knows her from, so he says, "Do you know me?" To which she replies, "I think you're the father of one of my kids."

Now he thinks back to the only time he has been unfaithful to his wife and says, "My God, are you the stripper from my bachelor party that I laid on the pool table with all my buddies watching, while your partner spanked me with wet celery and then stuck a carrot up my ass?"

She said, "No, I am your son's math teacher."

A blonde goes to a doctor's office and asks the nurse if she has any grapes. The nurse says, "This is a doctors office we don't have any grapes." The blonde apologizes and leaves.

The next day she returns and again asks for grapes. The nurse says, "Madam, we don't have any grapes."

She returns for 5 straight days, asking for grapes each time. On the 5th day the nurse barks, "The next time you come here and ask for grapes I will staple your feet to the floor!"

The next day the blonde comes back and says "Excuse me nurse, do you have any staples?"

The nurse has just about had it with her and snaps, "No, I do NOT have any damn staples!"

The blonde asks, "In that case, do you have any grapes?"

8

Corny Jokes

This short chapter is guaranteed to illicit many groans and not the "good" kind either. But if you accidentally left this book within arms reach of your young child, this is the one chapter you can rest assured that they can read without Child Protection Services having to get involved. My kids will probably have CPS on speed dial but that's another story. Anyway, these jokes & puns are really corny. I'm apologizing up front…

A blind man walks into a store with his seeing-eye dog. All of a sudden, he picks up the leash and begins swinging the dog over his head. The manager runs up to the man and asks, "What are you doing?!!"
The blind man replies, "Just looking around."

Two jumper cables walk into a bar and order a drink. The bartender says, "I'll serve you, as long as you don't start anything."

A guy walks into a bar with a piece of asphalt under his arm. He says to the bartender, "Hey, give me one for the road."

Sir Lancelot and Sir Galahad stopped at a roadside lemonade stand. The owner said, "I'm sorry but I can only give one of you a glass." Perplexed, they asked, "Why? What's the problem?"
The owner replied, "This is just a one-knight stand!"

Hear about the guy born with no arms, no legs, no torso or no head; just an eye? The sad part was that he was blind.

My girlfriend had sex with a midget... I can't believe she's stoop that low!

Corny Q&A

Q: Did you hear the joke about the toilet?
A: Never mind it's too dirty

Q: What did one toilet say to the other toilet?
A: You look flushed.

Q: What happened when the wheel was invented?
A: There was a revolution.

Q: What does a ghost call his mother & father?
A: Trans-parents.

Q: What did the teddy bear say when he finished eating?
A: Man, I'm stuffed!

Q: If 2 is a couple & 3 is a crowd, what's 4 & 5?
A: Nine.

Q: What did one chimney say to the other?
A: Mind if I smoke?

Q: Why did the coach send in his 2nd string?
A: He wanted to tie up the game.

Q: Do you like raisin bread?
A: Don't know; I never raised any.

Q: How does a man on the moon get his hair cut?
A: Eclipse it.

Q: Why do florescent lights always hum?
A: They don't know the words.

Q: Why can't a man living in the USA be buried in Canada?
A: 'Cuz he's still alive.

Q: Some months have 31 days. How many have 28?
A: All of them.

Q: How can you tell that a right angle is educated?
A: It has 90 degrees.

Q: Why did the man run around his bed?
A: He was trying to catch up on his sleep.

Q: Why can't you send a telegram to Washington?
A: He's dead.

Q: Do they have a 4th of July in England?
A: Yes, they also have a 2nd, a 3rd, a 5th...

Q: Where can you find an ocean with no water?
A: On a map.

Q: What's the difference between a drunk and an alcoholic?
A: A drunk doesn't have to go to those stupid meetings.

Q: What happened when the two silkworms raced?
A: They ended up in a tie.

Q: What side does a leopard have the most spots?
A: The outside.

Q: What the definition of an "Ex-King?"
A: One who's come in & out of the reign.

Q: What did the pony say when it had a sore throat?
A: I apologize, I am a little horse!

Q: What did the baby corn ask the mama corn?
A: Where's pop corn?

Q: What did the mayonnaise say when someone opened the refrigerator door.
A: Close the door; I am dressing!

Q: What happened when two peanuts were walking down the street?
A: They were a-salted.

Q: What do you call a cow with no legs?
A: Ground beef.

Q: Do you know who sounds like an owl?
A: Who?

Q. Why does a seagull fly over the sea?
A. Because if it flew over the bay it would be a bagel.

Q: Did you hear about the restaurant on the moon?
A: Great food but no atmosphere...

Q. Why is there a gate around cemeteries?
A. Because people are dying to get in.

Q: Hear about the blind hooker?
A: Hey, you've gotta hand it to her...

Q: What do you call a Mexican with a rubber toe?
A: Roberto

Q: What do you call an Asian lawyer?
A: Chop Suey

(I actually wrote this one and tried it onstage one night. My comedian buddy, Paul D'Angelo, told me if I ever did another joke this horrifically corny he would punch me in the face. I never uttered it again. I hope this doesn't count Paulie! lol)

My Resume

- My first job was working in an Orange Juice factory, but I got canned. I just couldn't concentrate.

- Then I worked as a Lumberjack, but I just couldn't hack it, so they gave me the axe.

- After that, I was a Tailor, but I just wasn't suited for it. It was a sew-sew job anyway.

- Next, I tried working in a Muffler Factory, but that was too exhausting.

- Then I tried to be a Chef - figured it would add a little spice to my life, but I just didn't have the thyme.

- I attempted to be a Deli Worker, but any way I sliced it, I couldn't cut the mustard.

- My best job was a Musician, but eventually I found I wasn't noteworthy.

- I studied a long time to become a Doctor, but I didn't have any patience.

- Next, I worked in a Shoe Factory. I tried, but I just didn't fit in.

- I became a professional Fisherman, but discovered that I couldn't live on my net income.

- I had a job working for a Swimming Pool Company, but the work was just too draining.

- So then I landed a gig at a Workout Center, but they said I wasn't fit for the job.

- After many years of trying to find steady work, I finally got a job as a Historian until I realized there was no future in it.

- My last job was working in Starbucks, but I eventually quit because it was always the same old grind.

- So, I tried retirement and, you know what? I'M PERFECT FOR THE JOB!

Corny Philosophy

Don't sweat the petty things and don't pet the sweaty things.

One tequila, two tequila, three tequila, floor...

Atheism is a non-prophet organization.

If man evolved from monkeys and apes, why do we still have monkeys and apes?

I went to a bookstore and asked the saleswoman, "Where's the self-help section?" she said, "If I told you it would defeat the purpose."

What if there were no hypothetical questions?

If a deaf person signs swear words, does his mother wash his hands with soap?

Is there another word for synonym?

Where do forest rangers go to "get away from it all?"

What do you do when you see an endangered animal eating an endangered plant?

If a parsley farmer is sued, can they garnish his wages?

Would a fly without wings be called a walk?

Why do they lock gas station bathrooms? Are they afraid someone will clean them?

If a turtle doesn't have a shell, is he homeless or naked?

Can vegetarians eat animal crackers?

If the police arrest a mime, do they tell him he has the right to remain silent?

Why do they put Braille on the drive-through bank machines?

How do they get deer to cross the road only at those yellow road signs?

What was the best thing before sliced bread?

One nice thing about egotists: they don't talk about other people.

Does the Little Mermaid wear an "algebra?"

Do infants enjoy infancy as much as adults enjoy adultery?

How is it possible to have a civil war?

If one synchronized swimmer drowns, do the rest drown too?

If you ate both pasta and antipasto, would you still be hungry?

If you try to fail, and succeed, which have you done?

Whose cruel idea was it for the word "lisp" to have an "s" in it?

Shouldn't hemorrhoids be called "ass-teroids?"

Why is it called tourist season if we can't shoot at them?

Why is there an expiration date on sour cream?

If you spin an oriental person in a circle three times do they become disoriented?

Can an atheist get insurance against acts of god?

I wondered why the baseball was getting bigger. Then it hit me.

Police were called to a day care center where a three-year-old was resisting a rest.

Did you hear about the guy whose whole left side was cut off? He's all right now.

The roundest knight at King Arthur's round table was Sir Cumference.

The butcher backed up into the meat grinder and got a little behind in his work.

To try writing with a broken pencil is pointless.

When fish are in schools they sometimes take debate.

The short fortune teller who escaped from prison was a small medium at large.

A thief who stole a calendar got twelve months.

A thief fell and broke his leg in wet cement. He became a hardened criminal.

Thieves who steal corn from a garden could be charged with stalking.

We'll never run out of math teachers because they always multiply.

When the smog lifts in Los Angeles: U.C.L.A.

The math professor went crazy with the blackboard. He did a number on it.

The professor discovered her theory of earthquakes was on shaky ground.

The dead batteries were distributed free of charge.

If you take a laptop computer for a run it could jog your memory.

A dentist and a manicurist fought tooth and nail.

A bicycle can't stand alone; it is two tired.

A will is a dead giveaway.

Time flies like an arrow; fruit flies like a banana.

A backward poet writes inverse.

In a democracy it's your vote that counts; in feudalism, it's your Count that votes.

A chicken crossing the road: poultry in motion.

If you don't pay your exorcist you may get repossessed.

Show me a piano falling down a mine shaft and I'll show you A-flat miner.

When a clock is hungry it goes back four seconds.

The guy who fell onto an upholstery machine was fully recovered.

You are stuck with your debt if you can't budge it.

Local Area Network in Australia = The LAN down under.

He broke into song because he couldn't find the key.

A calendar's days are numbered

A lot of money is tainted: "Taint yours, and 'taint mine."

A boiled egg is hard to beat.

He had a photographic memory which was never fully developed.

A plateau is a high form of flattery.

Those who get too big for their britches will be exposed in the end.

When you've seen one shopping center you've seen a mall.

If you jump off a Paris bridge, you are in Seine.

When she saw her first strands of gray hair, she thought she'd dye.

If someone with multiple personalities threatens to kill himself, is it considered a hostage situation?

9

Sports & Fitness

Are you in the shape you want to be? Do you live you life vicariously through your favorite sport teams? Did you pick up on the fact that each of the preceding questions had nothing to do with the other one? If you answered "yes," "no," or "both" to each then you somehow reasoned, in your head that they actually do. In reality, that's how the mind of an "arm-chair quarterback" works.

C'mon, admit it; you know you're out of shape but you still show up every Sunday at the bar wearing your favorite team's football jersey and/or hat, as if your participation could somehow affect the outcome of the game. We're all slaves to our beloved teams, regardless of our current physical conditions (which we all deem fit enough to do better than the players on the field at any given time). Then, we sober up and the next day realize that, not only are we incapable of performing athletic feats at such an elite and professional level, but we also grasp the fact that we are in such pitiful shape that we even get winded doing Kegel Exercises – with a spotter!

Before we get to the workout, you know we have to stretch out and get loose. To get you warmed up, I'll begin with some of the most brilliant philosophy since Socrates.

Top 5 Yogi Berra Quotes

"We made too many wrong mistakes."

"I usually take a two-hour nap from 1 to 4."

"No wonder nobody comes here; it's too crowded."

"Baseball is 90 percent mental. The other half is physical."

"Always go to other people's funerals, otherwise they won't come to yours."

An old, out of shape guy was working out in the gym when he spotted a sweet young thing. He asked the trainer, "What machine should I use to impress that sweet young thing over there?"

The trainer looked him up and down and said, "For you? I'd try the ATM machine!"

Three women are dressing in a country club locker room. Suddenly, a naked guy runs by wearing nothing but a bag over his head. He passes the first woman, who looks down at his penis. "He's not my husband," she says.

He passes the second woman, who also looks, "Well, he's certainly not my husband either." she says, also not recognizing the unit.

As he passes the third woman, she looks down and says, "Wait a minute, he's not even a member of this club!"

A Packers fan wound up with really crappy seats at Lambeau Field. Through his binoculars, he spotted an empty seat on the 50-yard line so he made his way down. When he arrived there, he asked the man in the next seat if the empty one was taken.

The man replied, "This was my wife's seat. She was a big Packers fan. She recently passed away."

The other man replied, "I'm so sorry to hear of your loss. May I ask why you didn't give the ticket to a friend or relative?"

The man sighed, "They're all at her funeral."

One of the younger guys at a construction site was bragging that he could out-do anyone in a feat of strength. He made a point of singling out the oldest guy. He kept it up until the old guy had enough.

"Why don't you put your money where your mouth is?" the old guy demanded. "I bet you a week's pay that I can wheel something in a wheelbarrow over to that building that you won't be able to wheel back."

"You're on, old man!" the young braggart replied.

The old guy grabbed the wheelbarrow by the handles, nodded to the young guy, and said, "All right, dumb-ass. Get in."

St. Peter and Satan were having an argument one day about baseball. Satan proposed a game to be played on neutral grounds between a select team from God and his own hand-picked boys. "Very well," said St. Peter. "But I hope you realize that we've got all the good players and coaches."

"Yeah I know, that's fine." Satan answered unperturbed. "But we've got all the umpires."

Coming home from his first Little League game, Billy swung open the front door very excited. Unable to attend the game, his father immediately wanted to know what happened. "So, how did you do son?" he asked.

"You'll never believe it Dad!" Billy said. "I was responsible for the winning run!"

"Really? How'd you do that?"

"I dropped the ball."

Two buddies, Bob and Earl, were two of the biggest baseball fans in America. They spent their entire lives discussing baseball history in the winter and poring over box scores during the season. They went to 60 games a year. They even agreed that whoever died first would try to come back to inform the other if there actually was baseball in heaven.

One August night, Bob passed away in his sleep after watching the Red Sox victory earlier that evening. He died happy. A few nights later, Earl awoke to the sound of Bob's voice from beyond.

"Bob, is that you?" Earl asked.

"Of course it me." Bob replied.

"This is unbelievable! So tell me, is there baseball in heaven?"

"Well, I have some good news and some bad news. Which do you want to hear first?"

"Tell me the good news first."

"Well, the good news is that yes, there is baseball in heaven, Earl."

"Oh, that is wonderful! So what could possibly be the bad news?"

"You're pitching tomorrow night."

A doctor ordered a chubby fellow to lose 75 pounds. So he ordered the 3-Day/10 lb Weight Loss System. The next day at his door appeared a beautiful, 19 yr. old babe wearing only sneakers & a sign around her neck saying, "If you can catch me, you can have me." So he takes off after her. A few miles later, huffing and puffing, he catches up and has his way with her.

The next two days, the same girl shows up and the same thing happens. On the fourth day he weighs himself and, sure enough, he lost 10 pounds. Intrigued by the company's workout methods he orders their new 5 Day/20 lb. System.

The next day he opens his door and is greeted by a knock-out babe, hotter than the last one, wearing only sneakers and a sign, "If you can catch me, you can have me." He quickly darts after her but she's in such good shape it takes a while to catch her. When he does, it's worth every cramp & wheeze and he has his way with her.

Over the next four days the same girl shows up and the same thing happens. On the last day he weighs himself, finding he's shed another 20 pounds. Elated, he calls the company and orders the 7-Day/50 lb. System. The sales rep asks, "Are you sure, sir? This is our most rigorous program."

"Most definitely; I love your program! It's worked for me every time. Bring it on!" he said.

The next day at his door appears a 250 lb. greasy, ex-con biker wearing only racing spikes and a sign, "If I catch you, your ass is mine!"

Q: What do you call a drug ring in Dallas?
A: A huddle.

Fore!!!!

Q. What's the difference between a G-Spot and a golf ball?
A. A guy will actually search for a golf ball.

A pro spent hours teaching a woman how to golf. Finally he sent her out to play on her own. When she returned he asked her how it went. She said, "Pretty good but, I got stung by a bee between the first two holes." The pro responded, "Well, that's probably because your stance was too wide!"

A man staggered into a hospital with a concussion, multiple bruises, two black eyes, and a five-iron wrapped tightly around his throat. The doctor asked him, "What happened to you?"

"Well," he replied, "I was having a quiet round of golf with my wife. At a difficult hole, we both sliced our balls into a pasture. We went to look for them, and while I was looking around, I noticed one of the cows had something white sticking out of its rear end. I walked over, lifted its tail, and sure enough, there was a golf ball stuck right in the middle of the cow's ass. I was pretty sure it was my wife's. Still holding the tail up, I yelled to her, 'Hey, this looks like yours!' I don't remember much after that."

The 16th hole featured a long fairway that ran beside a main road. Pooch, the first one of the foursome to tee off, hooked the hell out of his drive. The ball soared over a fence and bounced onto the street, hit the tire of a moving bus and ricocheted back onto the fairway mere yards from the green.

As they all stood in amazement, one of the guys asked, "How the hell did you do that!!??"

Pooch confidently beamed, "You gotta know the bus schedule!"

Tom was growing impatient teaching his wife, Keri, to golf at a posh resort lined with million dollar mansions. On the third tee he begged, "Whatever you do, don't slice! I can't afford to pay for any damages for estates like those." Sure enough, she took a mighty swing and shanked the ball right through the living room window of the biggest house on the course. "Dammit Keri, look what you've done now! Let's go see how much this is going to cost me."

They knocked on the door, and heard, "Come in." They entered and saw broken glass all over and a broken bottle lying next to the coffee table. "Sir, I'm terribly sorry. What do I owe you?"

"Owe me?" he laughed, "You don't understand; I'm a genie. See that vase lying on the floor? I've been trapped inside it for 1000 years. You saved me. I'm allowed to grant 3 wishes. I'll give you each one wish and, if you don't mind, I'll keep the last for myself."

Elated, Tom asked, "How about $10 million dollars?" "No problem!" said the genie and snapped his fingers, "Done. It's in your bank account now. Then he turned to Keri, "And you?" She replied, "I'd love a beautiful beach house on each coast." The genie snapped his fingers, "Done!"

"So what's your wish genie?" asked Tom. "Well, it's been so long since I've been with a woman, could I make love your wife, just once, to break this 1000-year curse?"

Tom looked at his wife, "Well honey, he did make us set for life. One time couldn't hurt." She agreed and the genie led Keri upstairs where he ravished her for hours – far better than she'd ever gotten from Tom.

When they finally finished, basking in the afterglow of the best sex either of them ever had, the guy lit a cigarette and asked, "How old did you say your husband was?" "45" Keri replied.

He laughed, "And he still believes in genies? Fucking remarkable!"

A golfer is playing a horrible round by himself when out of the woods pops a leggy young blonde asking, "Do you mind if I finish playing with you?" "Yes I do." She responded, "You look tense. I'll tell you what, let me play with you and I'll give you the best blowjob you've ever had!" Who could turn that down? So she takes him behind a tree and smokes his pole like a pro.

He goes on to play the best round in his life, beating his best score by 10 strokes.

The next day, he's back playing worse than ever when on the same hole, out pops the same blonde. "Give you another hummer if you let me golf with you." He agrees and she leads him behind a tree and blows him better than before. He then went on to break the course record.

This happened everyday for a week. Everyday she blows him then finishes golfing with him. Finally he says, "Lady, this has been the best week of my life. I'm golfing better than ever and I owe it all to you. Let me return the favor and go down on you before we play today."

The blonde says, "I'd love that! But, there's something you should know... I'm actually a transvestite." His face reddens, blood boiling, he finally explodes; "And I let you hit from the fucking ladies tees!?!?"

John sliced his ball into the woods and it landed in a patch of buttercups. Trying to get it back in play, he ended up thrashing just about every buttercup in the patch. Suddenly in a cloud of smoke, "POOF!" a little old woman appeared and said, "I'm Mother Nature! Do you know how long it took me to make those buttercups? Just for that you won't have any butter for the rest of your life. Not for popcorn, toast, corn on the cob... nothing!" Then "POOF" she simply vanished and John called out to his gold buddy, "Hey Fred, where are you?"

Fred yells back, "John, I'm over here. I hit my ball into the pussy willows."

John yells back, "Don't Swing, Fred!!! For the love of God, don't swing!!!"

Three friends play golf together every Saturday. One day they were getting ready to tee off when a random guy asked if he could join them. They all agreed and promptly teed off. A few holes in, they asked him what he did for a living.

The stranger claimed he was a hit man. They nervously chuckled. He said, "No, seriously; I really am a hit man. In fact, my rifle is in my golf bag right now. Go ahead and take a look, if you don't believe me."

So one of the guys opened the bag and sure enough, there was a rifle with a scope on it. He said, "WOW! I bet I can see my house through here! The stranger said, "Go ahead and try it."

He looked through the scope and said, "YEAH! I can even see through my windows into my bedroom. There's my wife, naked. WAIT! There's my next-door neighbor! He's naked too!"

Upset, he asked the hit man how much his service would cost. He replied, "Its $1,000 every time I pull the trigger." The man said, "$1,000? Okay. I want two hits:

1) Shoot my wife right in the mouth. She's always bitching and I can't stand it.

2) I want you to shoot my neighbor right in the dick, for screwing around with my wife."

The hit man agrees, lifts the rifle and looks through the scope. After a few minutes the man starts getting impatient and finally asks the hit man, "Hey, what are you waiting for?"

He replies, "Just hold on...I'm gonna do this with one bullet and save you a thousand bucks!"

A woman is taking a golf lessons at a local country club. The pro instructs her to "hold the club like it's your husband's penis." So she swings away and the ball dribbles 10 yards from the tee.

The pro says, "Okay, not bad. Now try taking the club out of your mouth!"

Two strangers are paired up on the course one day. As one guy is about to chip onto the green, he sees a long funeral procession on the road next to the course. He stops in mid-swing, takes off his golf cap, closes his eyes, and bows down in prayer.

The other guy says, "Wow that is one of the most thoughtful and touching things I have ever seen. You are truly a kind man."

He sighs, "Yeah, well, we were married 35 years."

A priest, a doctor, and a lawyer were stuck behind a tremendously slow foursome of golfers. After a few holes, they complained to the greens keeper. He explained, "Sorry guys, but that's a group of blind firefighters who lost their eyesight saving our clubhouse from burning down last year, so we decided we should let them play free rounds of golf anytime they want."

"That's very sad." the priest lamented. "I'll say a special prayer for them tonight."

The doctor said, "I'll contact my ophthalmologist pal to see if he can do anything for them."

The lawyer sighed, "That's all good and well but c'mon, can't they play at night?"

Best Caddy Comments

Golfer: I'd move heaven and earth to break 100 on this course.

Caddy: Try heaven, you've already moved most of the earth.

Golfer: Do you think my game is improving?

Caddy: Yes sir, you miss the ball much closer now.

Golfer: Do you think I can get there with a five iron?

Caddy: Eventually.

Golfer: You've got to be the worst caddy in the world.

Caddy: I don't think so sir. That would be too much of a coincidence.

Golfer: Please stop checking your watch all the time. It's too much of a distraction.

Caddy: It's not a watch - it's a compass.

Golfer: Do you think it's a sin to play on Sunday?

Caddy: The way you play, sir, it's a sin on any day.

Golfer: That can't be my ball, it's too old.
Caddy: It's been a long time since we teed off, sir.

Golfer: I Think I'm going to drown myself in the lake.
Caddy: You think you can keep your head down that long?

Jumpin' on the Bandwagon

The following are classic interchangeable sports jokes – just change the player or team name to suit your needs. Guess where I'm from?

Alex Rodriguez walked into the doctor's office and said, "Doc, I've got a problem. Now please, you've got to promise me that you won't laugh!" The doctor says, "Of course I won't laugh. I'm a professional. In over twenty years, I've never once laughed at any of my patients."

"Okay then." he says, and proceeds to drop his pants, revealing the tiniest penis, including infants, the doctor had ever seen. So small, in fact, it was almost invisible to the naked eye.

Unable to control himself, the doctor starts giggling and then finally begins laughing hysterically. After a few minutes he managed to regain his composure just enough to catch his breath and wipe away the tears from his eyes.

Embarrassed, the doctor says, "A-Rod, I'm so sorry! I really am. I don't know what came over me. On my honor as a doctor, a scholar, and a gentleman, I promise it will not happen again! Now, what seems to be the problem?"

A-Rod sighs, "It's swollen."

A minister decides to travel around America. He's at a beach in New England looking out at the water. Suddenly, he sees a man in a Yankees cap being attacked by a shark. The minister starts to panic, but then he sees two men in a boat, both wearing Red Sox caps, pull the man and the shark into the boat. When they come to the shore, the minister commends the Red Sox fans for their kindness and bravery, and how they'll surely be rewarded in heaven. He says he was proud of them for putting baseball's biggest rivalry and behind them. When the minister blesses them and walks away, one Red Sox fan turns to the other and says, "So—how's the bait doing?"

God was giving Jets coach Rex Ryan a tour of heaven. He showed him a little run-down shack with a faded Jets banner hanging from the front porch and said, "This is your new home, Coach. Most people don't get their own house up here." Rex looks at the shanty then turns around to see the one on the top of the hill; a huge mansion with marble columns and plush patios under each window. New England Patriots flags line the sidewalks and windows with a huge Blue, Silver and Red Patriots banner hanging between the marble columns.

"God" he said, "let me ask you a question; why do I get this little house with a torn Jets banner and Bill Belichick gets a huge mansion with Patriot's banners and flags flying all over the place?"

God smiled for a moment then replied, "That's not Bill's house, that's mine."

A mid-western man decided to write a book about Churches around the country. He started in San Francisco and worked east from there. Going to a very large church, he began taking photographs and making notes.

He spotted a golden telephone on the vestibule wall and was intrigued by the sign which read: "Calls: $10,000 a minute." Puzzled, he asked the pastor who then explained that the golden phone is, in fact, a direct line to heaven and, if he pays the price, he can talk directly to God. He thanked the pastor and continued on his way.

While visiting churches in Seattle, Dallas, St. Louis, Chicago, Milwaukee, etc. he found more phones with the same sign and the same answer from each pastor. Finally, he arrived at a church in Boston and, upon entering he saw the usual golden telephone with a sign: "Calls: $.35 cents."

Fascinated, he asked the pastor, "Your holiness, I've been in churches all across the country and have been told this golden telephone is a direct line to God in Heaven. But all of those phones cost $10,000 a minute. Yet here it's only $.35 cents a call. Why is that?"

Smiling benignly, the pastor said, "Son, you're in Boston now, home of the Red Sox, Patriots, Celtics, Bruins, and BC! -- You're in God's Country; it's a local call!"

10

Animals

Ever notice how pet owners always say, "My dog is the cutest dog in the world!" Look, I can understand taking pride in your animal but let's be real; anyone who says that is absolutely delusional and clearly in denial. The fact is that my dog Truckee really is the cutest dog in the history of the universe. I have proof. Deal with it!

Whether you own one or have been forced to see an abandoned one on a late night infomercial starring Sarah McLachlan, we all have come into contact with animals at some point in our lives. One look into their precious eyes and you can't deny that they don't have a soul. They aren't just a part of our lives; they are an integral extension of us. Why wouldn't they have thoughts akin to ours? I say, they do. The following jokes prove just that!

Two flies are sitting on a piece of shit. One cuts a huge fart. The other fly shoots him a dirty look and says, "Hey come on, I eating here!"

Two fleas met every winter in Miami for a vacation. Last year when one flea got there he was shivering and shaking. The other flea asked, "Why are you shaking so badly?" He says, "I rode down here from New Jersey in the moustache of a guy on a Harley."

The other flea says, "You should try what I do: Go to the airport bar and look for a nice stewardess. Crawl up her leg and nestle in her pubic hair where it's warm and cozy. It's the best way to travel." The flea replies, "Wow, thanks! I'll definitely give it a try next winter."

The next year the first flea showed up in Miami shivering and shaking again. The second flea asks, "Didn't you try what I told you?" "Yes," he says. "I did exactly as you said. I went to the airport bar, had a few drinks, and finally this beautiful stewardess came in. I crawled right up into her pubic hair. It was so nice and warm that I fell asleep. When I woke up, I was back in the moustache of a guy on a Harley."

Three Labrador retrievers are in the waiting room at the vet's office. The black lab turns to the brown lab and says, "So why are you here?" The brown lab replies, "I'm a digger. I dig under fences, dig up flowers, dig up carpets... And I crossed the line last night when I dug a huge hole in my owner's couch."

The black lab says, "So what is the vet going to do?"

"Give me Prozac," said the brown lab. "All the vets are prescribing it. Guess it works for everything."

The black lab turns to the yellow lab, "Why are you here?"

He replies, "I'm a pisser. I piss on everything; the sofa, the drapes, the cat, the kids... But the final straw was when I pissed on my owner's bed."

The black lab asked, "So what are they going to do to you?"

"Looks like Prozac for me too." the yellow lab lamented. The yellow lab then asked the black lab why he's there.

"I'm a humper." he says. "I hump the cat, the table, fire hydrants, the kids... I hump everything I see. Yesterday, my owner just got out of the shower and was bent over drying her toes, and I just couldn't help myself – I hopped on her back and started humping away."

The yellow and brown labs exchange sad glances and say, "So Prozac for you too, huh?"

The black lab says, "No, I'm just here to get my nails clipped."

A Mountain Lion is on top of a hill fucking a Zebra. He's really going at it with her when out of the corner of his eye he spots his wife, Mrs. Mountain Lion, coming up the hill. She's about to catch him red-handed.

Thinking quickly, the Mountain Lion grabs the Zebra by the shoulders and whispers in her ear, "Hey, quick. Act like I'm killing you!"

An eagle swoops down and swallows up a frog. The frog works his way around awhile, pokes his head out the eagle's ass and says, "Man, how high up you think we are?"

The eagle says, "We gotta be a thousand, two thousand feet up."

The frog says, "You ain't shittin' me now, are ya'?"

A grasshopper hops into a bar. The bartender says, "Hey, you want to know something? You're actually quite the celebrity around here. We even have a drink named after you!"

The grasshopper replies, "Really? You've got a drink named Steve?"

Two dogs are walking by a parking meter. One turns to the other and says, "How do ya' like that? Pay toilets!"

One day a bear ran into a rabbit in the middle of a forest and said, "Hey, let me ask you a personal question. Do you ever have problems with shit sticking to your fur?"

The rabbit responded, "No, not at all!" "Oh good!" said the bear as he promptly picked up the rabbit and wiped his ass his him.

Young Johnny is walking through the park with his father and sees two dogs humping. "Hey dad, what are they doing?" His father says, "Son, they're making a puppy."

Later that night, young Johnny walked into his parent's room and saw them going at it, "Hey dad, what are you doing?" He said, "Son, we're making you a baby brother."

Johnny says, "Yeah, well flip her over. I'd rather have a puppy!"

A woman passes the same pet store everyday on her way to and from work. One day, a parrot perched on a roost outside cawed, "Hey lady!" "Yes?" she replied.

"You're ugly and you have a fat ass!" Disgusted, she walked off.

On her way home that night, the same parrot cawed, "Hey lady!" "What?!" she said. The parrot replied, "You're ugly and you have a fat ass!" Incensed, she stormed away.

This happened everyday for a week. Finally, she'd had enough. She marched up to the owner, "Everyday I pass your store and that damn parrot of yours tells me I'm ugly and have a fat ass. If this happens one more time, I'm going to sue you!"

The owner replied, "I'm terribly sorry, Ma'am. I'll talk to

him and I promise this will never happen again!" Satisfied, she left.

The next day on her way to work she passed the store again and, sure enough, the parrot balked, "Hey lady!" She snapped, "WHAT?!"

The parrot just winked at her and said, "You know!"

Two guys; one a pessimist, the other an optimist, had been friends for years. The optimist was always trying to get his pal to see the positive side of things but, it was always to no avail.

One day the optimist found a dog that could walk on water. He thought, "This is perfect! There's no way that damn cynic could possibly say anything negative about this."

So he took his friend hunting so he could see the dog in action. Mid-morning, they shot a bird. It fell on the far side of a lake, so the optimist sent his dog to retrieve the bird. The amazing canine trotted right across the lake, grabbed the duck, and then returned, walking on top of the water.

The optimist said, "Isn't that amazing?"

The pessimist scoffed and shrugged his shoulders as he replied, "That dog can't even swim, can he?"

Petra was baking a birthday cake for her 13-yr. old son, Donny. While reaching for the sprinkles, she accidentally grabbed a container of BBs that she hid from Donny. Not realizing her mistake until later, she figured it would be okay, as the BBs would pass naturally. A while after the birthday celebration young Tami came running downstairs, "Mommy, I was going to the potty and BBs came out!"

"I know dear, you'll be fine now," said Mom.

Then young Sally came down, "Mommy, I was going number one and BBs came out."

Mom replied, "I know dear, it was an accident but everything's okay.

A little while later, Donny came flying in to the kitchen, "Mommy, mommy---"

She interrupted, "I know dear, you were going to the bathroom and BBs came out."

"No" he cried, "I was jerking off and I shot the dog!"

A little farm boy comes down to breakfast and his mother asks if he had done his chores. "Not yet." he said. His mother says, "Well, no breakfast until your chores is done!" So he left in a huff. He was so pissed he kicked a chicken when he went to feed them. Then he went to feed the cows and he kicked one. He goes to feed the pigs, and he kicks a pig. He heads back in for breakfast and his mother gives him only a bowl of dry cereal.

"Hey, how come I don't get any eggs and bacon? Why don't I have any milk in my cereal?" he asks.

"Well," his mother replies, "I saw you kick a chicken, so you don't get any eggs for a week. I saw you kick the pig, so you don't get any bacon for a week either. I saw you kick the cow so for a week you aren't getting any milk!

Just then, his father came down for breakfast and kicked the cat halfway across the kitchen. The little boy looks up at his mother with a smile and says, "You gonna tell him or should I?"

An old farmer was having a tough time getting his bull to breed with the cows. So his friend gave him some advice; "Whatcha' do is dip your finger into the cows vagina then, rub it under the bull's nose and he'll take right after her."

So the old man did just that, and like clockwork, the bull

got a rip roaring woody and mounted the cow. Later that night, the old farmer was lying in bed with his wife and he wondered if the same technique would work with his old unit. As she lay sleeping, he dipped his fingers into her box then, rubbed it all around his nose, and got an instant boner. He shook his wife awake, "Honey, look!"

She rolled over, turned on the light and said, "You woke me up in the middle of the night just to show me you have a nosebleed?"

Two worms are living together on a golf course. One says to the other, "Hey, I wonder what it's like outside today? Maybe I'll go up and check it out." So he starts heading up the tunnel.

Just as he's about to reach the surface, two lady golfers happen by. One says, "Geez, I've gotta go pee." Her friend replies, "No one is around, why don't you just go squat in the bushes?" So she looks around, pulls down her pants and starts peeing just as the worm pops his head out right below her. She completely soaks the poor worm from head to tail. So he quickly heads back down the tunnel.

When the drenched worm gets home, the other worm says, "I see it's raining, huh?"

He replies, "Hell yeah! In fact, it's raining so hard the birds are building their nests upside down!"

Two guys were walking their dogs. One had a Doberman and the other had a Chihuahua. As they sauntered down the street, the guy with Doberman said, "Let's go over to that bar and get a drink." His friend replied, "We can't go in there. We've got dogs with us." The guy with the Doberman said, "Relax. Just follow my lead."

So he put on a pair of dark glasses, started to walk in and was immediately stopped by the bouncer. "Sorry Mac, no pets allowed." The man said, "But you don't understand, this is my Seeing-Eye dog." The bouncer was skeptical, "A Doberman Pinscher?" The man said, "Yes, they're very good." The bouncer muttered, "Well okay, come on in."

Next, the guy with the Chihuahua put on a pair of dark glasses and started walking in, only to be stopped by the bouncer. "Sorry pal, no pets allowed!" The man with the Chihuahua said, "But Sir, you don't understand, this is my Seeing-Eye dog." The bouncer said, "Come on, a Chihuahua?"

He shrieked, "A Chihuahua? Those bastards gave me a fucking Chihuahua?!"

A teacher is explaining biology to her 4th grade students. "Human beings are the only animals that stutter." she says. A little girl raises her hand, "I had a kitty-cat who stuttered." The teacher was curious and asked the girl to describe the incident.

"Well," she began, "I was in the back yard with my kitty and the Rottweiler that lives next door got a running start and before we knew it, he jumped over the fence into our yard!"

"That must've been scary!" said the teacher.

"It sure was!" said the little girl. "My kitty raised his back, went 'Ffffff, Ffffff, Ffffff' and before he could say 'Fuck' the Rottweiler ate him!"

The LAPD, The FBI, and the CIA were trying to prove who was best at apprehending criminals. So the President gave them a test: he released a rabbit into a forest and each of them has to catch it. The CIA goes in first. They place animal informants throughout the forest and question all plant and mineral witnesses. After three months of extensive investigations they conclude that rabbits do not exist.

The FBI goes in next. After two weeks with no leads they burn the forest, killing everything in it, including the rabbit, and they make no apologies, "Hey, the rabbit had it coming."

Then the LAPD goes in. They come out two hours later with a badly beaten bear. The bear is yelling, "Okay! Okay! I'm a rabbit! I'm a rabbit!"

A man walks into a bar with an ostrich and a cat. The bartender says, "What can I get for you?" The man says, "I'll have a beer." The ostrich says, "I'll also have a beer." The cat says, "I'll have half a beer and I'm not buying." The bartender says, "Okay, that'll be $9.87."

The man reaches into his pocket and brings out the exact change and pays him.

Later, the bartender returns, "Ready for another round?" The man and the ostrich say, "I'll have a beer" and the cat says, "I'll have half a beer and I'm not buying." The bartender brings their beer and says, "That'll be $9.87." The man reaches into his pocket and brings out the exact change and pays him.

A few days later they return to the bar and the bartender asks, "What'll ya' have today?" The man says, "I'll have a scotch." The ostrich says, "I'll have a bourbon." And the cat says, "I'll have half a beer and I'm not buying." The bartender says "That'll be $15.53."

Again, the man brings out the exact change and pays him. The bartender's curiosity got the best of him and he asks, "How do you always have the exact change in you pocket?"

The man said, "I found a genie in a bottle and was granted 3 wishes. My 1st wish was to always have the exact change in my pocket for anything I buy."

The bartender says, "That's a great wish! A million dollars will run out but that never will. What were your other two wishes?"

The man sighs, "That's where I screwed up. I asked the genie for a chick with long legs and a tight pussy."

A mama mole, a papa mole, and a baby mole all live in a little mole-hole. One day the papa mole sticks his head out of the hole, sniffs the air and says, "Yum! I smell maple syrup!"

The mama mole sticks her head out of the hole, sniffs the air and says "Yum! I smell honey!"

The baby mole tries to stick his head out of the hole to sniff the air, but can't because the bigger moles are in the way so he says, "Geez, all I can smell is.... MOLASSES!"

Two tall trees; a birch and a beech, are growing in the woods. A small tree begins to grow between them, and the beech says to the birch, "Is that a son of a beech or a son of a birch?" The birch says he cannot tell. Just then a woodpecker lands on the sapling.

The birch says, "Woodpecker, you're a tree expert. Can you tell if that is a son of a beech or a son of a birch?" The woodpecker takes a taste of the small tree and replies, "My friends, it is neither a son of a beech nor a son of a birch. It is, however, the best piece of ash I have ever stuck my pecker in."

Two woodpeckers, one from Hawaii and one from California, were arguing about which place had the toughest trees. The Hawaiian woodpecker claimed that Hawaii had a tree that no woodpecker could peck. The Californian woodpecker accepted his challenge and promptly pecked a hole in the tree with no problem. The Hawaiian woodpecker was in awe.

Not to be outdone, the California woodpecker then challenged the Hawaiian woodpecker to peck a tree in California that was absolutely im-peckable (pun intended…). The Hawaiian woodpecker was confident he could do it so he accepted the challenge and flew to California where he successfully pecked the tree with no problem.

So the two woodpeckers were now confused. How is it that the California woodpecker was able to peck the Hawaiian tree and the Hawaiian woodpecker was able to peck the tree in California but neither one was able to peck the tree in their own state?

After much woodpecker-pondering, they came to the same conclusion: Your pecker is always harder when you're away from home!

Some race horses were in a stable when one of them starts to boast about his track record. "In the last 15 races, I've won 8 of them!" Another horse chimes in, "Well in the last 27 races, I've won 19!" "Not bad, but I've won 28 of my last 36 races!" says another, flicking his tail.

At this point, they notice that a greyhound has been sitting there listening in. "I don't mean to boast," says the greyhound, "but in my last 90 races, I've won 88 of them!"

The horses are clearly amazed. "Wow!" says one, after a hushed silence. "A talking dog!"

Recently, the Psychic Friends Network launched a hotline for frogs. One day a frog called in and one of the psychics claimed, "You are going to meet a beautiful young girl who will want to know everything about you."

The frog says, "This is great! Will I meet her at a party, or what?"

"No," says the psychic. "Next semester in her biology class."

One cold, snowy night a couple was driving along when they hit a skunk. The wife, an avid animal lover, begged her husband to stop the car. He begrudgingly obliged and she hopped outside, picked up the nearly lifeless skunk, and carried him back to the car, placing him on the passenger's side floor.

"He's still breathing. Maybe we can get him to the vet on time?" she said. "Look dear, he's shivering. He's probably freezing to death. What should I do?"

"Try holding him between you legs. That should warm him up." he replied.

"But what about the smell?" she asked.

Without missing a beat he said, "Just hold his little nose!"

Two guys went moose hunting every winter without success. Finally, they came up with a foolproof plan; they got an authentic female moose costume and learned the mating call. They planned to hide in the costume, lure the moose, then come out and shoot it. They set up on the edge of a clearing, donned their costume and began to give the moose love call.

Before long, a bull came crashing out of the forest and into the clearing. When the bull was close enough, the guy in front said, "Okay, let's get out and get him." After a moment, the guy in the back shouted, "Oh shit, the zipper is stuck! What the hell are we going to do?"

The guy in the front says, "Well, I'm going to start nibbling grass, but you'd better brace yourself!"

Two whales were swimming off the coast of Japan when

they noticed a whaling ship. The male recognized it as the same ship that had harpooned his father many years earlier. He said to the female, "Let's swim under the ship and blow out of our air holes. That should cause the ship to turn over and sink." They tried it and sure enough, the ship turned over and quickly sank.

Soon however, they realized the sailors had jumped overboard and were swimming towards safety. The male was enraged that they were going to get away and told the female, "Let's swim after them and gobble them up before they reach the shore."

The female, reluctant to follow him, said, "Look, I went along with the blow job, but I absolutely refuse to swallow seamen!"

Animal Q & A

Q: What do you call a female turtle?
A: A Clitortoise.

Q: What do you get when you cross a cat with a dog?
A: A pussy that comes when you whistle.

Q: On which side does a leopard have the most spots?
A: On the outside.

Q: What happened when two silk worms were in a race?
A: They ended up in a tie.

Q: How do you stop a charging rhino?
A: Take away his credit cards.

Q: Why did Beethoven get rid of his chickens?
A: They kept saying, "Bach, Bach, Bach..."

Q: If fruit comes from a fruit tree, what kind of tree do chickens come from?
A: A poul-tree.

Q: Two flies are on the porch; which is the actor?
A: The one on the screen.

Q: Why did the monkey fall out of the tree?
A: Because he was dead!

Q: What the toughest part about having sex with a sheep?
A: Having to walk all the way around front to kiss him goodbye.

Q: What do you call a guy with his hand up a horse's ass?
A: An Amish mechanic.

True Story!

There were three flies in a jar; two female and one male. One of the females asks the male, "Do you know a way to get out?" The male fly replies, "Suck my dick and I'll tell you!"

So she did and the male told her to fly up to the top of the jar and hit the lid real hard. She did this and fell back down dead.

The second fly then begs the male, "Please, you must tell me how to get out!" He replies, "Suck my dick and I'll tell you!" She does so and again, the male instructs her to fly up to the top of the jar and hit the lid two times real hard. She too did this and fell back down dead.

Want to know how the male fly got out? Suck my dick and I'll tell you!

11

Music

If you've made it this far into the book it should be pretty obvious that I don't get offended easily and it's damn near impossible to shock me. Yet when it comes to poking fun at musicians I must admit I get a little squeamish as I am incredibly passionate about music. I started playing drums when I was 10 and picked up the guitar years later. I played throughout high school and in several college bands.

One gimmick we tried was calling our band "Free Beer." Tons of people would show up but quickly get pissed off when they found out the beers weren't actually "free." One of my college groups actually won the "Battle of the Bands" and, as a result, we got to open up for Scandal. (Yes, the "Shootin' at the walls of heartache, bang, bang… I am the warrior!" Scandal.) Sure, we went on at 6pm and they didn't gig until 9pm, and we never got the chance to meet them but it's still a cool credit, right? Hello… is this thing on?

I honestly believe most musicians don't get the credit they deserve. Unless you have learned an instrument yourself, you have no idea how much time & practice it takes even just to become "adequate" at it. We've got armadillos in our pants… yes; I'm riffing to kill some time here as it'll be a short chapter. Regardless, these jokes are funny and, sadly, true for the most part. Enjoy…

Will the musicians & the drummer please come to the stage?!

Q: What do you call a guitar player that only knows two chords?
A: A music critic.

Q: What do you call a guitar player without a girlfriend?
A: Homeless.

Q: What do you call a guitarist's girlfriend?
A: A relative minor.

Q: What do you call a beautiful woman on a guitar player's arm?
A: A tattoo.

Q: What does a guitarist say when he gets to his gig?
A: Would you like fries with that?

Q: What's the definition of a successful guitarist?
A: A guy whose girlfriend has 2 jobs.

Q: What is the difference between a guitarist and a Savings Bond?
A: Eventually a Savings Bond will mature and earn money!

Q: What's the difference between a guitarist and God?
A: God doesn't think he's a guitarist.

Q: What is the difference between a piano and a tuna fish?
A: You can tune a piano but you can't tuna fish. (REO Speedwagon, anyone???)

Q: What's the difference between a banjo and an onion?
A: Nobody cries when you chop up a banjo.

Q: Why do some people have an instant aversion to banjo players?
A: It saves time in the long run.

Q: What's the difference between a folk guitar player and a large pizza?
A: A large pizza can feed a family of four.

Q: What's the difference between a chick singer and a pit bull?
A: Lipstick.

Q: What will you never say about a keyboard player?
A: "That's the keyboard player's Porsche."

Q: How many trumpet players does it take to pave a driveway?
A: Seven- if you lay them out correctly.

Q: What's the difference between an oboe and a bassoon?
A: You can hit a baseball further with a bassoon.

Q: What's the difference between a dead chicken and a dead trombonist in the road?
A: There's a remote chance the chicken was on its way to a gig.

Q: What's the definition of optimism?
A: A flute player with a beeper.

Q: How do you reduce wind-drag on a bass player's car?
A: Take the Domino's Pizza sign off the roof.

Q: How do you get a bass player off of your porch?
A: Pay him for the pizza.

Q: What do you throw a drowning bass player?
A: His amp.

Q: How do you get a three-piece horn section to play in tune?
A: Shoot two of them.

Q: What do you call a musician with a college degree?
A: Night manager at McDonalds.

Q: How do you define a perfect pitch?
A: When the accordion lands in the middle of the dumpster.

Q: What's the last thing a drummer says before he gets kicked out of a band?
A: "So when do we get to play my songs?"

Q: How can you tell if the stage is level?
A: The drool comes out of both sides of the drummer's mouth.

Q: How many deadheads does it take to change a light bulb?
A: 12,001. One to screw it in, 2,000 to bootleg-record the event, and 10,000 to follow it around until it burns out.

Q: How many musicians does it take to change a light bulb?
A: Twenty - 1 to hold the bulb, 2 to turn the ladder, and 17 to be on the guest list.

Q: How many folk musicians does it take to change a light bulb?
A: Seven; one to change and the other six to sing about how good the old one was.

Q: How many drummers does it take to screw in a bulb?
A: None, they have machines for that now.

Q: How many drummers does it take to change a light bulb?
A: 20. One to hold the bulb and 19 to drink until the room spins.

Q: How do you know when a drum solo's really bad?
A: The bass player notices.

Q: What's the definition of a perfect gentleman?
A: Somebody who knows how to play the accordion, but doesn't.

Q. How is playing a bagpipe like throwing a javelin blindfolded?
A. You don't have to be very good to get people's attention.

Q. Why do bagpipers leave their cases on their car dashboards?
A. So they can park in handicapped zones.

Q: How do you tell when your lead singer is at the door?
A: He can't find the key and doesn't know when to come in.

Q: What do you get when you play a new age song backwards?
A: A new age song.

Q: What happens when you play country music backwards?
A: You get your job, your truck, your dog, and your wife back.

Q: How many guitar players does it take to cover a Stevie Ray Vaughn tune?
A: Evidently all of them.

Eric Clapton and Jerry Garcia are captured by cannibals. They tell them they can have a last request before being killed and eaten. Jerry Garcia says, "I'd like to play Truckin' one more time." Eric Clapton says, "Can you kill me first?"

A man walks into a shop and asks, "Hey dude, do you got one of them Marshall Hi-watt, AC30 amplificatior thingies and a Gibson Strato-Blaster with a Fried Rose tremolo?"
The salesman says, "You're a drummer, aren't you?"
"Yeah, how'd you know?"
"This is a travel agency."

U2 are doing a concert in Ireland when Bono asks the audience for some quiet. In the silence, Bono starts slowly clapping his hands. Holding the audience in total silence, Bono says into the microphone, "Every time I clap my hands, a child in Africa dies."

A voice from the crowd pierces the silence... "Then stop clappin' yer fookin' hands!!!"

Three men die and go to heaven and are greeted by St. Peter. He asks the first guy, "Hi, what's your name?"

"My name is Paul."

"Nice to meet you Paul. Tell me, when you died, how much were you earning?"

"About $120K per year."

"Wow! Paul, what were you doing to earn that kind of money?"

"I was a lawyer."

"That's great. Come on in!"

St. Peter then turns to the second man, "Hello there. And what's your name?"

"I'm Roger."

"Hi, Roger. Tell me, when you died, how much were you earning?"

"About $75K each year."

"Nice! So what did you do for a living?"

"I was a tax accountant."

St. Peter said, "Well, that's very good! Come on in."

Then St. Peter turned to the last man, "Hi, and you are?"

"My name is John."

"Hi, John. So John, how much were you earning when you died?"

"Well, I only made about $7,000 in my lifetime."

"I see. Well John, what instrument did you play?"

A jazz musician dies and goes to heaven. St. Peter tells him, "Hey man, welcome! You've been elected to the Jazz All-Stars of Heaven; right up there with Satchmo, Miles, Django, all the greats... We have a gig tonight. Only one problem; God's girlfriend gets to sing!"

A sax player dies and goes to the pearly gates. St Peter says, "Sorry but you partied too much on earth. You have to go to hell." The elevator doors open and he enters a huge bar where the greatest musicians ever are on stage during a break. He goes over to Jimi Hendrix and says, "Hey this can't be hell; all the best are playing here!" Kurt Cobain turns to him and says, "No dude, Karen Carpenter is on drums!"

A trombone player and an accordion player are doing a New Year's Eve gig at a local club. The place is packed and everybody absolutely loves the music. Shortly after midnight, the club owner comes up to the duo and says, "You guys are amazing! Everybody loves you! I'd like to book you back here right now for next New Year's Eve. Are you open?

The two musicians nod to each other then look at the club owner. Then the trombone player says, "Sure, we'd love to! Is it okay if we leave our stuff here?"

A man bought his wife a piano for her birthday. A few weeks later, their son called to see how she was doing. "Oh," said the father, "I persuaded her to switch to the clarinet."

"How come?" the son asked.

"Well," he answered, "because with a clarinet, she can't sing...."

A father bought guitar lessons for his son. The 1st week

he asked him what he had learned. The son said, "In my 1st lesson we learned all about the E string." After the second the lesson the father again asked what he learned. He said, "Pop, today I learned all about the A string."

The third week came and the father said, "You know son, these lessons are very expensive. I certainly hope you're learning more than just playing 2 strings! What did you learn this week?"

The son said, "Fuck the lessons Pop, I already got a gig!"

A guy walks into a doctor's office and says, "Doc, I haven't had a bowel movement in weeks!" The doctor gives him a prescription for a mild laxative and says, "If this doesn't work, let me know." A week later the guy came back, "Doc, still no movement!" The doctor says, "Hmm, guess you need something stronger." and prescribes a powerful laxative.

Still another week later the poor guy is back, "Doc, still nothing!" The doctor, worried, says, "Perhaps I should get some more information about you to try to figure out what's going on. What do you do for a living?"

"I'm a musician."

The doctor looks up and says, "Well bingo, that's it! Here's $10. Go get something to eat!"

A mind reader is at a nightclub one night and decides to test her skills on the band playing. First, she reads the mind of the lead guitarist: "Wow, look at all the hot chicks that showed up tonight! I'm gonna get laid!"

Then she reads the drummer's mind: "We're killing! This is great!"

Next, the Keyboard player: "These guys have no appreciation of my talent. What a bunch of losers!"

Finally, she reads the Bass player's mind: "C...G...C...G..."

Two drummers and a violinist formed a band. During a gig one night, the sound is just awful. One drummer turns to the other and says, "Man, we sound terrible. I don't think this is going to work. Let's get rid of the fucking violinist!"

A musician calls the symphony office to talk to the conductor. "I'm sorry, he's dead." is the reply. The musician calls back 25 times, always getting the same reply form the receptionist. At last she asks him why he keeps calling. "I just like to hear you say it!"

A young boy says, "Mom, when I grow up I'd like to be a musician." She replies, "Well honey, you know you can't do both."

Fearing an Indian attack was imminent, two cowboys kept watch over their circled-wagon party. Then, in the darkness, they began to hear the beating of a war drum. One cowboy turns to his partner, "Man, I really don't like the sound of those drums!"

Suddenly, an Indian taps him on the shoulder and whispers, "He's not our regular drummer!"

(One of my all-time, personal favorites!!!)

So you think you've got what it takes to be a musician? Be forewarned; it's harder than it looks. Let's see if you have the chops. And you don't have to spend thousand's of dollars on equipment either. I'll get you started with only your phone

(Rotary phones excluded. If you still have one of those then go ahead and take yourself out of the gene pool by shooting yourself in the temple!) Here's a classic jingle that can easily be played just by pushing the right buttons. C'mon, give it a shot. You just might want to quit your day job!

Mary Had A Little Lamb - 3212333, 222, 399, 3212333322321

12

The Island of Misfit Jokes

This chapter is a collection of random jokes that just didn't fall into any specific category or there weren't enough on a particular topic to fill a whole chapter. Or maybe I just got lazy and didn't feel like figuring out where to stick them in the book? Either way, I plugged 'em all here, in no particular order. Enjoy...

Confucius Say: "Schoolboy who fool around with schoolgirl during wrong period get caught red-handed..."

Confucius Say: "Man who walk through airport turnstile sideways going to Bangkok."

A musician was paid handsomely score a movie. Though he never saw a script, he still managed to write some beautiful music. Three months later, he receives notice that the movie will debut in Times Square at a seedy porno house. He reticently accepts the invitation.

Embarrassed, he enters the theatre wearing a dark raincoat, a brimmed hat, and shades.

Unaccustomed to porno flicks, he sits in the last row next to an elderly couple. The film has explicit sex scenes: oral and anal intercourse, golden showers, dirty Sanchez's, sado-masochism and, in the final scene, the female lead has incredibly graphic sex with a dog. The musician is mortified. He turns to the elderly couple and whispers, "I wrote the score for this film and I only came to hear my music."

The elderly woman whispers back, "We just came to see our dog."

Two little kids are in a hospital lying on beds next to each other outside the operating room. The first kid leans over and asks, "What are you in here for?"

The second kid says, "I'm in here to get my tonsils out and I'm a little nervous."

The first kid says, "You've got nothing to worry about. I had that done when I was four. They put you to sleep and when you wake up they give you lots of Jell-O & ice cream. It's a breeze."

The second kid then asks, "What are you here for?" The first kid says, "A circumcision." The second kid says, "Whoa, good luck with that, buddy. I had that done when I was born... couldn't walk for a year!"

A lady walks into a high class jewelry shop. Browsing around, she spots a beautiful diamond bracelet and, as she bends over for closer inspection, she inadvertently breaks wind. Embarrassed, she looks around to see if anyone noticed her "accident." As she turns, her worst nightmare is realized; a salesman is standing right behind her.

Displaying complete professionalism, he greets her with, "Good day, Madam. How may we help you today?" Very uncomfortable, but hoping that the salesman may just not have been there at the time of her little mishap, she asks, "Sir, what is the price of this lovely bracelet?"

He says, "Honey, if you farted just looking at it; you're gonna' shit when I tell you the price!"

(2 Great Jokes to Nail Your Friends - just insert their names)

Three midgets are sitting around one day trying to come up with ways that they can get in to the Guinness Book of World Records. The first midget says, "Ya' know, I bet I have the smallest hands in the world. I think I'll go check it out." So he goes to the Guinness office and, sure enough, he's got the smallest hands in the world. He runs back to his tiny friends, waving the Guinness Book, "Look, look, I made it; smallest hands in the world!"

His friends congratulate him and sing his praises. The 2nd midget says, "Ya' know, I bet I have the smallest feet in the world. I think I'll go check it out." So he heads to the office and, wouldn't you know, he's got the smallest feet in the world. He returns, waving the Guinness Book, "Hey guys, check it out, I got in: smallest feet in the world!!!" They all celebrate.

Finally, the third midget says, "Well, I guess it's my turn. This is a little embarrassing but I bet I have the smallest penis in the world. It's not even a 1/4 inch, fully erect." His mini peers squeaked, "Hey, as long as it gets you in the Guinness Book of World Records, who cares? Go for it!"

Determined, he went to the office. An hour later he returns, dejected, head hung low... He holds the Guinness Book up to his wee friends, wipes a tear from his eye and says, "Guys, who the hell is Woody Cunrod?

(Tell this one in the first person)

Hey guys, I had this dream last night that Carlson, Wayne, and I died and went to heaven. St. Peter was giving us a tour and led us into this one huge room full of clocks. I mean thousands of them, all set at different times, all with different people's names above them. So I had to ask, "St. Peter, what's with all these clocks?"

St. Peter replied, "Well Rick, this is our way of keeping track of the sinners down on earth. Every time one of you masturbated, your clock moved ahead by five minutes." We all laughed and went to look for our clocks. I found mine; it was like 7:30. A little while later, we found Carlson's, it was set around the stroke of midnight. After searching all over the room however, we couldn't find Wayne's clock.

So he pulled St. Peter aside and asked, "excuse me St. Pete but, we've been looking all around here and we can't seem to find my clock. Is there a problem?" St. Peter smiled, "No Wayne, your clock is in my office. I was using it as a fan!"

A very unattractive, mean woman walks into Wal-Mart with her two kids. She has a nasty looking tattoo on each arm and rotten teeth. To make it even worse, she's wearing flip flops and has long, filthy toenails. The Wal-Mart greeter asks, "Are they twins?" The ugly bitch says, "No, the oldest one is 9 and the younger is 7. Why? Do you think they look alike?" "No," replies the greeter, "I just can't believe you got laid twice!"

"I've got some good news and some bad news," the doctor says. "What's the bad news?" asks the patient. "The bad news is that unfortunately you've only got 3 months to live." The patient is taken back, "Well what's the good news?"

The doctor points over to the secretary at the front desk, "You see that blonde with the bedroom eyes, big breasts, tight ass, and long sexy legs?" The patient shakes his head, "Yeah…"

The doctor smiles, "I'm fucking her!"

A very sexually active woman tells her plastic surgeon that she wants her vaginal lips reduced in size because they were loose and flapping. Out of embarrassment she insisted that the surgery be kept a secret and the surgeon agreed. Awakening after the surgery she found three roses carefully placed beside her on the bed.

Outraged, she immediately calls in the doctor. "I thought I asked you not to tell anyone about my operation!" The surgeon told her he had carried out her wish for confidentiality and that the first rose was from him citing, "I felt bad because you went through this all by yourself." "The second rose is from my nurse. She assisted me in the surgery and empathized because she had the same procedure done some time ago."

"And what about the third rose?" she asked. He replied, "That was from a man upstairs in the burn unit. He wanted to thank you for his new ears!"

A man fell asleep on the beach and suffered severe sunburn to his legs. His skin turned bright red and started to blister. Anything that touched his legs caused agony. He was taken to the hospital where the doctor prescribed intravenous feedings of water and electrolytes, a mild sedative and Viagra. Astounded, the nurse inquired, "What good will Viagra do in his condition?"

The doctor replied, "It'll keep the sheet off his legs!" Mrs. Jones goes to the doctor for a full medical. After examining her for a bit, the doctor says, "Mrs. Jones, I do see one slight problem: you are roughly 45 pounds overweight so I suggest that you start dieting right away to avoid any complications in your later years."

Appalled and angered she glares at him and says, "Well, I demand a second opinion!!!"

"Okay," he says, "you're fucking ugly as well!"

This beautiful, sexy young woman was at the doctor's office. He asked to disrobe and climb onto the examining table. "Doctor," she replied shyly, "I just can't undress in front of you."

"All right," said the physician, "I'll turn off the lights. You undress and tell me when you're through."

In a few moments, her voice rang out in the darkness, "Doctor, I've undressed. What shall I do with my clothes?"

"Put them on the chair, on top of mine."

A man is sitting in the Doctor's Office. The doctor looks up from his paperwork, takes off his glasses then rubs his eyes. "Sir, you really have got to stop masturbating!"

The man says, "But why?" The doctor exclaims, "So I can examine you!!!"

A couple met at a bar and hit it off so well that they decided to go to the girl's place. A few drinks later, one thing led to another, the guy takes off his shirt and then washes his hands. He then takes off his trousers and washes his hands again.

The girl has been watching him and says, "You must be a dentist." Surprised, the guy says, "Yes, how did you figure that out?"

She replied, "Easy, you keep washing your hands." They

make love and after they finish the girl says, "You must be a good dentist."

The guy, now with boosted ego, says "I'm a damn good dentist. How did you figure that out?"

She smiles wryly, "Because I didn't feel a thing!"

A little boy is shopping with his mother and waiting for her to come out of the dressing room. Bored, he slides his hand up a mannequin's skirt. His mom comes out and catches him. "Get your hand out of there!" she shouts. "Don't you know women have teeth down there?"

The little boy snatches his hand away, relieved he didn't get bitten. The boy grows up believing all women have teeth between their legs. When he's 16, he gets a girlfriend. One night while her parents are out, she invites him over for a little action. After an hour of making out and grinding she says, "You know, you could go a little further if you want."

"What do you mean?" he asks. "Well, why don't you put your hand down there?" she suggests.

"No way!" he cries. "You've got teeth down here!"

"Don't be ridiculous, there's no such thing!" "Yes, there is. Mom told me so." "Here, see for yourself."

Then she pulls down her pants, gives him a little peek and says, "See? No teeth."

The boy takes a good long look, inspecting every inch. "Well, after seeing the condition of those gums, I'm not surprised!"

A crusty old biker out on a summer ride in the country pulls up to a tavern in the middle of nowhere. Passing thru the swinging doors, he sees a sign: COLD BEER: $2.00 - FRENCH FRIES: $2.25 - CHEESEBURGER: $2.50 - HAND JOB:

$50.00 Checking his wallet to be sure he has the necessary funds, he walks up to the bar and beckons the exceptionally attractive female bartender.

She smiles, "May I help you?" The biker leans over the bar and whispers, "I was wondering if you are the pretty young lady who gives the hand jobs?" She looks into his eyes with a wide smile and purrs, "Why yes, I sure am." He leans closer and says, "Well, go wash your hands real good, 'cuz I want a cheeseburger!"

A guy noticed that his waiter had a spoon in his shirt pocket. Then he looked around and saw that all the staff had spoons in their pockets. When the waiter came back with his food he asked, "What's with the spoon?" He explained, "Well, a consulting team concluded that the spoon is the most frequently dropped utensil so if we are better prepared, we can drastically reduce the number of trips back to the kitchen and save a minimum of five man-hours per shift."

The guy was impressed. Then he also noticed there was a string hanging out of the waiter's fly. Sure enough, he noticed all the waiters had string hanging from their flies. Again he asked, "Why do you have that string right there?" The waiter whispered, "They also found that we can save bathroom time by tying this string to the tip of you-know-what so we can pull it out without touching it and eliminate the need to wash our hands, shortening the time spent in there by 76%.

The guy asked, "Okay, but after you get it out, how do you put it back without touching it?"

"Well," he whispered, "I don't know about the other guys, but I just use the spoon!"

A guy was struggling to decide what to wear to a fancy

costume party. Finally, came up with a bright idea and proceeded to get ready. When the host answered the door, he found the guy standing there wearing only a pair of jeans; no shirt, socks or shoes. "What the hell are you supposed to be?" asked the host.

"A premature ejaculation." said the man. "I just came in my pants!"

A young Texan goes off to college, but 1/2 way through the semester he foolishly squandered all the money his parents gave him. Then he got an idea and called home, "Dad, you won't believe the wonders of modern education they're coming up with! They actually have a program here that'll teach our dog, Truckee, how to talk!"

"That's absolutely amazing," his father says. "How do we get him in that program?"

He replies, "Just send him down here with $1,000 and I'll get him into the course."

So, his father sends the dog and the money. A few weeks later the money runs out again so the boy calls home again. "How's Truckee doing, son?" his father asks.

"Awesome Dad, he's talking up a storm! But you won't believe this - they've had such good results that they've implemented a new program to teach them how to read!"

"READ?!?! No kidding! What do I have to do to get him in that program?"

"Just send $2,500 and I'll get him in the class."

Once again, his father sends the money but, the boy now has a serious problem: at the end of the year, his father will find out that the dog can't either talk or read. So he shoots the dog.

When he gets home at the end of the semester, his father is all excited.

"Where's Truckee? I just can't wait to see him talk and read something!"

The boy says, "Dad, I have some grim news. Yesterday morning, just before we left to come home, Truckee was in the living room reading the newspaper as usual. Then he turned to me and asked, 'Hey is your father still messing around with that little redhead who lives on Oak Street?' So dad, I had to shot that old SOB before he talked to Mom!"

"Son, you did the right thing!"

A young boy asks his father, "Dad, what is the difference between potentially and realistically?" He thought for a moment then said, "Go ask your mother, sister, and brother if they'd sleep with Brad Pitt for a million dollars. Come back and tell me what you learn."

So the boy asked his mother, "Would you sleep with Brad Pitt for a million dollars?" She replied, "Of course! We could use that money to fix up the house and send you kids to college!"

He then asked his sister, "Would you sleep with Brad Pitt for a million dollars?" She exclaimed, "My God, are you nuts? I'd sleep with him in a heartbeat!"

Finally, he asked his brother and he replied, "Sure dude, why not? You can buy a lot of stuff with a million bucks!"

The boy pondered for awhile and then went back to his dad. "So, did you find out the difference between 'potentially' and 'realistically'?"

The boy replied, "Yes, potentially, you and I are sitting on three million dollars. But realistically, we're living with two hookers and a queer!"

Three desperately ill men met with their doctor one day to discuss their options. One was an alcoholic, one a chain-smoker, and one a homosexual. The doctor, addressing all three, said, "If any of you indulge in your vices one more time, you will surely die." The men left the doctor's office; each convinced they'd never again indulge in their vices.

While heading toward the subway, they passed a bar. The alcoholic, hearing the loud music and seeing the lights, could not stop himself. His buddies accompanied him into the bar, where he had a shot of Whiskey. Just as he slammed the shot he fell off his stool, stone cold dead.

His companions, shaken, left realizing how seriously they must heed the doctor's words. Walking along, they spotted a cigarette butt lying on the ground, still burning. The homosexual looked at the chain smoker and said, "If you bend over to pick that up, we're both dead!"

A woman walks into a supermarket and buys a bar of soap, a toothbrush, a loaf of bread, a pint of milk, a box of cereal, a frozen dinner, a can of Soup, and a 16oz can of Miller Lite. The checkout guy says, "Single, are you?" She smiles, "Why yes, how did you guess?"

He replies, "Because you're ugly."

A young soldier calls home from the Army Reserves and says to his father, "Pop, yesterday they took us skydiving. I was last. I told the Sergeant I couldn't go because I was too scared.

He said to me, "Well son, I'm gay. And there's only one way you're getting out of it..."

His father asked, "So did you jump?"

He replied, "A little at first..."

A little old lady is walking down the street dragging two big garbage bags. There's a hole in one of them and once in a while a $20 bill flies out onto the street. A policeman stops her, "Ma'am, there are $20 bills falling out of that bag." "Darn!" says the little old lady. "I'd better go back and see if I can find them. Thanks for the warning!"

"Whoa, not so fast," he says. "How did you get all that money? Did you steal it?" She says, "Oh heavens, no! You see my back yard is next to the football stadium parking lot. Whenever there's a game; many drunken fans come and pee in the bushes behind my flower bed! So, I stand behind the bushes with hedge clippers and each time someone whips his thingy out I say, '$20 or off it comes!'"

"Hey, not a bad idea!" laughs the cop. "By the way, what's in the other bag?"

"Well," says the little old lady, "Not all of them pay..."

A man runs into a bar and says, "Give me twenty shots of your best single-malt scotch, quick!" The bartender pours the shots, lines them up on the bar, and the man downs them as fast as he can. The shocked bartender says, "Wow, I been here many years and I've never seen anyone drink so fast."

The man says, "You'd drink fast if you had what I have."

The bartender says, "Oh my God, I'm sorry. What do you have?"

The guy says, "Fifty cents!"

Two dwarfs go into a bar, pick up two prostitutes and take them to their separate hotel rooms. The first dwarf, however, is unable to get an erection. His depression is made worse by the fact that, from the next room, he hears his little friend shouting out cries of "Here I come again...

ONE, TWO, THREE... UP!" all night long.

In the morning, the second dwarf asks the first, "How did it go?" He mutters, "It was so embarrassing. I simply couldn't get an erection.

The second dwarf sighed, "You think that's embarrassing? I couldn't even get on the bed!"

A nursery school teacher asks her class if they can use the word 'definitely' in a sentence. A little girl says, "The sky is definitely blue." Teacher says, "Sorry, but the sky can be gray, white, or even red."

A little boy says, "Trees are definitely green."

The teacher replies, "Sorry, but in the autumn trees can be brown, orange."

Little Johnny says, "Do farts have lumps?"

The Teacher looks horrified, "Of course not Johnny!"

"Ok...then I DEFINITELY shit my pants..."

One day in class the teacher asked, "What's 2+2?" Johnny raised his hand and said, "That'd be motherfuckin' 4." The teacher said, "Johnny you can't use that kind of language in class!" and Johnny said, "Why motherfuckin' not?"

The teacher called his parents and asked them to come to school to discuss this matter. The next day they came in and the teacher told them how Johnny uses always foul language whenever she calls on him. She asked his parents, "What do you think of that?"

Johnny's mother turned to the teacher, "Then don't fuckin' call on him!"

Two 8yr old boys lived across the street from a brothel. Everyday they saw men knock on the door, go in, and eventually come out happy and smiling. One day they became curious and decided to see what was going on. The Madam answers the door, looks down at the boys, and they ask her why all these men enter and then, shortly after, leave so happy.

The Madam thinks for a moment, shrugs, and says, "Do you have 5 dollars?" Both boys dig into their pockets and come up with a total of 50 cents. She says, "Okay, that'll have to do," and she proceeds to lift her skirt and pull down her panties. She tells both boys to take a sniff, which they do. She closes the door and the kids proceed home.

About halfway down the block one boy turns to the other and says, "Ya' know Joey, I don't think I coulda' stood $5 dollars worth of that stench!"

After trimming a priest's hair the barber refused payment saying, "No, Father. You do God's work." The next morning the barber found a dozen bibles on his doorstep. A few days later a policeman came in for a haircut. Again, the barber did not charge him saying, "No officer, you protect and serve." The next morning he found a dozen donuts on his doorstep.

The next day a lawyer came in for a cut. Again, the barber did not charge him saying, "No counselor, you serve the justice system!" The next day on his doorstep stood a dozen lawyers.

The United Way realized they had never received a donation from the city's most prominent lawyer, so a volunteer rep paid a visit to his lavish office. He opened by saying, "Our research shows your annual income is over two million dollars yet, you don't give a penny to charity. Wouldn't it be nice for you to give back to your community through the United Way?"

He thinks for a minute, "Well, did your research also show

you that my mother is dying after a long, painful illness and has huge medical bills that exceed her ability to pay?" Embarrassed, the rep mumbles, "Um... no, we weren't aware of that."

Then the lawyer says, "Okay, well did it show that my brother is a blind, disabled veteran, confined to a wheelchair, and is unable to support his wife and six children?"

The stricken rep begins to stammer an apology, but is cut off again. "And did your research also show that my sister's husband died in car accident, leaving her penniless with a mortgage and three children; one who is disabled and another that has learning disabilities requiring a vast array of private tutors?" The humiliated rep says, "I'm so sorry, I had no idea."

The lawyer leans back in his chair and smugly says, "So, if I didn't give any money to them, what makes you think I'd give any to you?"

A beautiful young lady is on the witness stand and the judge says, "What happened?" She cried, "He dragged me into an alley, ripped my dress off, bent me over a garbage can, grabbed my breasts, pulled my panties down and... I don't even remember what happened next."

The judge snapped, "Make something up! Make something up!!!"

A blind man walks into a restaurant and sits down. The owner hands him a menu. "I'm sorry, but I am blind and can't read this. Just bring me a dirty fork from a previous customer; I'll smell it and order from there."

Confused, the owner walks over to a dirty pile, picks up a greasy fork and returns to the table. The blind man puts the fork to his nose and takes in a deep breath. "Ah yes, that's what I'll have; Linguini with Alfredo sauce."

"Unbelievable!" the owner says as he walks to the kitchen. He tells his wife Mary, the chef, what just happened. The blind man enjoys his meal and leaves.

Days later he returns and the owner brings him a menu again. "Remember me? I'm the blind man." "I'm sorry, I didn't recognize you. I'll bring you a dirty fork."

The owner retrieves a dirty fork and, after another deep breath, the blind man says, "That smells great, I'll take the Veal Scaloppini with broccoli." Once again, the owner walks away in amazement. He tells Mary that the next time he comes in he's going to test him.

When he returns the following week, the owner runs into the kitchen and says, "Mary, quick, rub this fork on your panties." She complies and hands the fork back. As the blind man sits down, the owner is ready and waiting. "Good afternoon sir, this time I remembered you and I already have the fork ready for you."

The blind man takes a deep whiff of the fork and says, "Mary works here?"

A patron says to a saloon bartender of a small, "Hey buddy, I'll bet you $10 bucks I can walk 6 feet away and pee in this bottle, which I'll leave here on the bar. I won't miss a drop. I won't even hit the rim; it'll go right in the bottle." The bartender shakes his head, "Impossible! You're on!"

So the guy walks 6 feet from his stool, drops his pants and pisses all over the bar, the stools and the floor. He doesn't even come close to hitting the bottle.

The bartender bursts out laughing and exclaims, "Ha! I knew you couldn't do it. Hand over my 10-spot!" As he hands him $10, a guy at the other end of the bar passes out. The bartender looks over then asks, "What happened to him?"

The guy replies, "Oh, he'll be alright. I just bet him $1000 that I could piss all over your bar and you'd laugh about it."

A lady walks into a bar and says, "Give me 5 shots of Jack Daniels." The bartender pours them and she slams them all in a row, stands up, and then falls flat on her face. While she's passed out, every guy in the bar screws her.

A week later, she returns and says, "Give me 5 shots of Jack Daniels." He does. She drinks them, falls flat on her face and every guy in the bar nails her again.

The next week she comes back. "Give me 5 shots of Tequila." The bartender replies, "But I thought you liked Jack Daniels?"

She said, "Not any more; ever time I drink it, it makes my pussy sore!"

One cold, snowy night a man was driving in Alaska when his car broke down. He called AAA and they sent a mobile repair truck. The service man checked under the hood for a few minutes then stood up, looked at the man and said, "Ya' know, it looks like you've blown a seal."

The man replies, "No, it's just frost on my moustache."

A man in his 40's and was out for a drive in his new BMW. The top was down, the breeze was blowing through what was left of his hair, and he decided to open her up. As the needle jumped up to 80 mph, he suddenly saw flashing red and blue lights behind him. "There's no way they can catch my BMW!" he thought and opened her up further. The needle hit 90, 100, 110...

Then the reality of the situation hit him. "What the hell

am I doing?" he thought and pulled over. The cop approached him, took his license, and examined it as well as the car. "Look, it's been a long day, it's the end of my shift, and it's Friday the 13th. I don't feel like more paperwork, so if you can give me an excuse for your driving I haven't heard before, you can go."

The guy thinks for a second and says, "Last week my wife ran off with a cop. I was afraid you were trying to give her back." The officer handed his license back and smiled, "Have a nice weekend,"

A plane full of passengers grows impatient waiting for the pilots to show up. Finally, they emerge and begin walking up to the cockpit. Both seem to be blind; sunglasses, white canes, bumping into passengers as they stumble down the aisle and fumble at the cockpit door. After they shut the door behind them, the engines start revving and the plane taxis down the runway.

The passengers are uneasy; whispering among themselves and looking desperately to the stewardesses for reassurance. As the plane rapidly accelerates, people begin panicking and praying, and as it gets closer to the end of the runway, they become more hysterical. With less than 20 feet of runway left, they scream hysterically. At the very last moment, the plane lifts off and is airborne. Up in the cockpit, the copilot breathes a sigh of relief and tells the pilot, "You know, one of these days the passengers aren't going to scream, and we won't know when to take off!"

A passenger in a taxi leans forward to ask the cabbie a question and taps him on the shoulder. The cabbie screams, loses control, nearly hits a bus, drives over a curb, and stops just inches from a plate glass window. After a moment of silence, the shaken cabbie turns to the passenger and says, "I'm sorry, but you scared the daylights out of me!" The passenger apologizes, saying she didn't realize that a mere tap on the shoulder could frighten him so much.

The cabbie says, "No, no, I'm sorry, it's my fault. This is my first day driving a cab... I've been driving a hearse for 35 years."

A woman goes to her boyfriend's parent's house for dinner. This is her first time meeting them and she's very nervous. During the meal she begins to feel a little discomfort, thanks to her nervousness and the broccoli casserole. The gas pains almost make her eyes water. With no other choice, she decides to relieve herself a bit and lets out a dainty little fart. It wasn't loud, but everyone at the table heard the "toot."

Before she even had a chance to be embarrassed, her boyfriend's father looked at the dog snoozing by the women's feet, and said, "Truckee!"

A couple minutes later, she was beginning to feel the pain again. This time, she didn't even hesitate. She let a much louder and longer fart rip. The father looked at the dog and yelled, "C'mon Truckee!" Once again she smiled and thought, "Phew!"

Minutes later she let another one rip. This fart rivaled a train whistle. Again, the father looked at the dog and yelled, "Dammit Truckee, get away from her before she shits on you!"

Donald Rumsfeld was giving George Bush his daily briefing and concluded by saying, "Yesterday, 3 Brazilian soldiers were killed." "Oh no!" the president exclaimed. "That's terrible!" His staff sat stunned at his display of emotion, nervously watching as the president slumped, his head in his hands. Finally, Bush looked up and asked, "How many is a brazillion?"

Dick Cheney was out duck hunting one morning and had to take a leak. He walked over to a tree and propped up his gun. Just then a gust of wind blew; the gun fell over and discharged, shooting him right in the nuts.

Several hours later, his doctor approached his bed-side, "Well sir, I have some good news and some bad news: The good news is that you'll be fine. The damage was only to your groin, there was very little internal bleeding, and we were able to remove all of the buckshot."

"What's the bad news?" Cheney asked. The doctor replied, "Well, there was extensive buckshot damage done to your penis. I'm going to have to refer you to my sister."

"Well I guess that isn't too bad," Cheney said. "Is your sister a plastic surgeon?"

"Not exactly..." answered the doctor. "She's a flute player in the Chicago Symphony. She's going to teach you where to put your fingers so you don't piss in your eye!"

A high school English teacher reminds her class of tomorrow's final exam. "I won't tolerate any excuses for you not being here tomorrow. I might consider a personal injury or illness, a death in your immediate family, or perhaps a nuclear attack, - but no other excuses whatsoever!"

A smart-ass in the back of the room raises his hand, "What would you say if tomorrow I said I was suffering from complete and utter sexual exhaustion?" The entire class does its best to stifle their laughter and snickering.

When silence is restored, the teacher smiles sympathetically at the student, shakes her head, and sweetly says,

"Well, I guess you'd have to write the exam with your other hand!"

Random Q & A

Q: Why don't cheerleaders in San Francisco wear short skirts?
A: 'Cuz when they sit down, their balls hang out.

Q: What do lesbians do when they're both menstruating?
A: Finger paint.

Q: How can you tell a macho woman?
A: She rolls her own tampons.

Q: What do you call a lesbian with big fingers?
A: Well hung.

Q: Why do lesbians have belly buttons?
A: They need somewhere to put the tartar sauce.

Q: What was the difference between Neil Armstrong and Michael Jackson?
A: Neil Armstrong walked on the moon. Michael Jackson fucked little boys.

Q: When was it bedtime at Michael Jackson's ranch?
A: When the big hand touched the little hand...

Q: Why do men find it difficult to make eye contact?
A: Tits don't have eyes.

Q: What is the difference between medium and rare?
A: Six inches is medium, eight inches is rare.

Q. Why do women rub their eyes when they get up in the morning?
A. They don't have balls to scratch

Q: What do you call a vegetarian with diarrhea?
A: A salad shooter.

Q: What do you call a gay guy's balls?
A: Mud flaps.

Q. Why do gay guys like ribbed condoms?
A. Better traction in the mud.

Q. What is the difference between a drug dealer and a hooker?
A. A hooker can wash her crack and sell it again.

Q: What's yellow and green and eats nuts?
A: Gonorrhea

Q: What's the definition of macho?
A: Jogging home from your own vasectomy.

Q. How can you tell if you're at a bulimic bachelor party?
A. The cake jumps out of the girl.

Q: Did you hear about the two gay judges?
A: They tried each other.

Q: What's the difference between a dead lawyer & a dead snake in the road?
A: There are skid marks in front of the snake.

Q: What's the difference between a lawyer and a hooker?
A: A hooker usually stops fucking you when you're dead.

Q: What do you call 1000 lawyers at the bottom of the ocean?
A: A good start.

13

Wrong, Just Simply Wrong

I can assure you the placement of this chapter had nothing to do with "saving the best for last." Quite the opposite actually - You see, I figured I'd bury them in the back of the book, hidden and out of the way. Truthfully, I hope most of you just skip this chapter. Seriously, you don't want to read these jokes. They are really, really sick, twisted and just plain wrong. I highly recommend you just go back and re-read another chapter or perhaps start in on another book. Dan Brown's The Lost Symbol is a real page turner. Maybe you could start in on that before the movie comes out?

This isn't some clever little ploy to spike your curiosity either. If you like these jokes, you may want to seek psychiatric help. (That means you, Uncle Woody!) But you're adults and I can't stop you. Should you decide to forge ahead, please remember what I said at the start of this book: I didn't write these jokes so don't kill the messenger! You've been warned!!!

Simply Wrong Q&A

Q: What's better than winning 3 gold medals at the Special Olympics?
A: Not being retarded.

Q: What's 18 inches long, stiff as a board, and drives women crazy?
A: Crib death.

Q: What's funnier than a dead baby?
A: A dead baby in a clown suit.

Q: What's the difference between a luxurious, fur rug and a pile of dead babies?
A: I don't lie down on a luxurious, fur rug when I'm masturbating.

Q: What's the leading cause of pedophilia?
A: Sexy children.

Q: What did the child molester say when he got out of prison?
A: "Man, I feel like a kid again!"

Q: What's black & blue and hates sex?
A: The 7 yr. old in my trunk.

Q: What's the difference between acne & a priest?
A: You're around 14 years old before acne comes on your face.

Q: How can you tell when children are being sexually abused?
A: When they won't use a pacifier unless it has a hair on it!

Q: How do you stop a crying baby?
A: Cum in its mouth.

Q: What did one pedophile say to the other pedophile when a six year old girl walked by?
A: "Wow, I bet she was really hot when she was younger!"

Q: What did the deaf, dumb, and blind kid get for Christmas?
A: Cancer.

Q: What do you do to a deaf, dumb, and blind girl after you rape her?
A: Break her fingers so she can't tell anyone.

Q: How does an Arkansas mother know her daughter is having her period?
A: Her son's dick tastes funny.

Q: Why do tampons have strings?
A: So you can floss after eating.

Q: What's the difference between menstrual blood and sand?
A: You can't gargle sand.

Q: How do you turn a fruit into a vegetable?
A: AIDS.

Q: What's the difference between Santa Claus and a Jew?
A: Santa Claus goes *down* the chimney.

Q: Why did Hitler commit suicide?
A: He saw his gas bill.

A guy is walking into the woods with a young boy. The boy says, "It's really scary out here." The guy says, "You're scared? I've gotta walk outta' here alone!"

A man buys several sheep, hoping to breed them for wool. After several weeks, he notices that none of them are getting pregnant, and calls a vet for help. The vet tells him he should try artificial insemination.

The guy doesn't have the slightest idea what this means but, not wanting to display his ignorance, only asks the vet how he will know when the sheep are pregnant. The vet tells him they when they stop standing and lie down to wallow in the grass, they are pregnant.

He hangs up and gives it some thought. He concludes that artificial insemination must mean he has to impregnate the sheep himself. So he loads them into his truck, drives them out into the woods, has sex with them all, then brings them back and goes to bed.

Next morning, he wakes and looks out at the sheep. Seeing that they are all still standing around, he concludes that the first try didn't take, and loads them in the truck again. He drives them out to the woods, bangs each sheep twice for good measure, then brings them back and goes to bed.

Next morning, he wakes to find the sheep still just standing around. "One more try," he tells himself, and drives them out to the woods again. He spends all day shagging the sheep then returns home and immediately falls asleep. The following morning he can't even raise his head off the pillow so he asks his wife to look out and tell him if the sheep are lying in the grass.

"No," she says, "they're all in the truck and one of them is honking the horn."

One evening a man was at home watching TV and eating peanuts. He'd toss 'em in the air and then catch them in his mouth. In the middle of catching one, his wife asked him a question.

As he turned to answer her, a peanut fell in his ear. He tried to dig it out but only wound up pushing it in deeper. He called his wife for assistance, and after hours of trying they became worried and decided to go to the hospital.

As they were ready to go out the do or, their 16 year old daughter came home with her boyfriend. After being informed of the problem, the boyfriend said he could easily get the peanut out. He told the father to sit down, then proceeded to shove two fingers up his nose and told him to blow hard. When the father blew, the peanut flew out of his ear.

The mother and daughter jumped for joy. The young man insisted that it was nothing. Once he was gone, the mother turned to the father and said, "Isn't that's wonderful! He's so smart! What do you think he's going to be when he grows older?"

The father replied, "From the smell of his fingers, I'd say our son in-law."

A 13 year old boy asks his father, "Dad, what does a pussy look like?" A little bewildered, he asks, "Um, before or after sex?" The boy says "Geez, I didn't know there was a difference? I guess tell me what they look like before sex."

The dad says, "Son, before sex; a vagina is like a beautiful red rose with soft red peddles. The smell, the taste, and the texture are so amazing that even the most brilliant poets in the world could not describe it accurately. It is truly a work of God!"

"Wow, cool!" says the son. "So, what does it look like after sex?"

His dad sighs, "Son, have you ever seen a bulldog eating mayonnaise?"

A guy in a pub tells his friend, "You won't believe what happened. I was taking a short cut along the railway track and I found a girl tied to it. I untied her and then we had sex over and over, all the positions, everything." His friend replies, "That's great: did you get a blow job?"

"No. I never found her head."

Mark was having his first experience with a hooker. As he was going down on her he found a small piece of roast beef lodged in her pubic hair. He quickly spit it out and went back to work. Moment's later; he bit into a chunk of broccoli, then a carrot, then a pea... Finally he sat up, "What's going on here? Are you sick?"

"No "she replied, "but the guy before you was."

A girl walks into her parent's room, sees her mom putting on a bra and asks, "Mommy, what are those?" She replies, "Honey, these are mommy's breasts." "Oh, when will I get those?" Her mother says, "In about 10 years, when you go through puberty."

Later she sees her father getting out of the shower, toweling off. "Daddy, daddy! What's that!?"

"Well, honey, this is daddy's penis." She asks, "Oh, when will I get one of those?"

The dad replies, "In about 10 minutes, when your mom goes to work!"

Little Timmy comes running in the back yard, "Pop, Pop... Mom just got run over and killed by a bus!" He said, "Son, you know my lips are chapped, please don't make me smile!"

Young Peter walked into the bathroom just as his mother was stepping out of the tub. He pointed to her crotch, "Mommy, Mommy, what's that?" Blushing, she replied, "Peter, this is Mommy's axe wound."

Young Peter responded, "Wow, right in the cunt!"

A man gets out of prison with only $5 to his name. He bolts to the nearest whorehouse. The Madam limps over to him, "May I help you?" He slaps the $5 on the counter, "Madam, I been in jail 15 years and, I know this ain't a lot of money but, you gotta help me out. My balls are so blue, I'm ready to bust wide open!" She sympathizes, "Okay, I get the picture. I will help you but, you've got to listen carefully; there's a woman in room #3 already waiting in bed, lights off, naked, legs spread... Go in there and do not turn the light on. Just hop on top of her, do your business, and get out." The man breaths a sigh of relief, "Thank you kindly Madam."

He runs down the hallway to room #3. He opens the door, feels his way over to the bed, takes his pants off, climbs on top of her and goes at it. It's been so long that he explodes instantly, shooting the biggest load of his life for what seems like an eternity.

Finished, his curiosity gets the best of him and he clicks the light on. His jaw drops as he sees the woman with cum dripping out of her mouth, out of her nose, her ears, her eye sockets - every orifice in her body.

He puts his pants on and sprints up to the Madam. "I don't know what happened but after I finished, this girl, well, she had my pecker snot oozing out of her eyes, her ears, her mouth..."

The Madam shakes her head and yells to the cleaning woman, "Juanita, the dead one in room #3 is full again!"

Two guys are walking down the street and see a dog on the lawn, licking his balls. One guy says, "Man, I sure wish I could do that."

The other guy says, "Don't you think you ought to pet him first?"

A pregnant woman was at the hospital giving birth to her baby. At long last, the doctor held up the newborn, cut the umbilical cord, and took a moment to look the baby over. Suddenly the doctor threw the child against the wall. The mother watched in horror as the baby slid to the floor with a sickening thud.

The nurses and orderlies stood-by aghast as the doctor proceeded to dribble the newborn around the room like a soccer ball before finally passing it through the door into the hall with a mighty kick. Everyone, including the mother, chased the doctor into the hall as he scooped up the infant and body-slammed him into the wall over and over.

At the end of the hall, the doctor gave a mighty leap and slam-dunked the baby into a nearby trashcan, giving himself a load roar of approval. Finally, the now large, awe-struck crowd caught up with the doctor. The mother was distraught and burst into tears.

"Why? Why in the name of God did you do that to my baby?" she cried.

The doctor replied: "Relax, I'm just joking with you! It was stillborn."

A guy is walking past a bus stop and says to a woman, "Can

I smell your pussy?" She yells back at him, "Fuck off, no you cannot smell my pussy!"

"Oh," he replies, looking slightly confused, "then it must be your feet!"

A guy was having sex with a girl, and decided he was going to try his luck, flip her over and do her doggy style. The girl didn't complain and just went along with it. The guy got a little more daring and decided to stick his finger in her ass. She still didn't say anything.

Then he decided to go all the way and proceeded to slip his dick in her asshole. The girl suddenly froze, looked back at him and said, "Don't you think it's a little bit presumptuous for you to think its okay to fuck me in the ass?"

He replied, "Wow! Presumptuous is a very big word for a five year old!!!"

While God is distracted, Eve persuades Adam to eat the forbidden fruit. He does so and they both realize they are naked! So they fuck each other madly all day long. Later, God appears and takes Adam aside for a stern talking-to about his sins.

When he's finished, he asks Adam where Eve went. "Oh, she's in the sea washing herself off," replies Adam.

"Oh fuck!" says God. "How am I ever going to get the smell out of the fish?"

A man asks a pharmacist for birth control pills for both his wife and his 7 year-old daughter. The pharmacist, quite shocked says, "Your 7 year-old daughter is sexually active?"

"No." sighs the man. "She just sort of lays there."

A Kentucky mother is making dessert after a family meal when her young son comes running in breathless. "Mom, Mom; quick! Granny is playing with her shrimp!"

Confused, she follows him into the dining room where the grandmother is furiously fingering herself.

"Ah!" said the mother. "Son, that's not a shrimp. That's actually called a vagina."

"Oh!" said the boy. "Well it certainly tasted like shrimp!"

CPSIA information can be obtained at www.ICGtesting.com
Printed in the USA
LVOW130922040912

297276LV00001B/4/P